Moscow Kremlin
Red Square

NEW GUIDE-BOOK

MOSCOW 2010

UDC 728.81(470-25)(036)=111

Under the editorship of I. Yudakov

Consultants:
V. Zakharov, Doctor of History
D. Grishin, Doctor of History
V. Petrushko, Doctor of Divinity
L. Uspenskaya , Chief scholar of State Historical Museum
A. Prokofieva, Associate scholar of State Historical Museum
M. Volpe

Computerized make-up: O. Erofeev

Publisher: I. Yudakov
e-mail: rogi13@mail.ru

Informational assistance:

State Historical
and
Cultural Museum-Preserve "The Moscow Kremlin"

Orthodox Society "Radonezh"
ОБЩЕСТВО
ꝰРАДОНЕЖꝰ

Technical assistance: Publishing house "Zebra E"
e-mail: zebrae@zebrae.ru
www.zebrae.ru

ISBN 978-5-904813-01-7

Immortal greatness of the Kremlin
Can't be expressed with mortal words!..
Nikolay Rubtsov, Russian poet

Contents

Foreword

Foreword

What is the Moscow Kremlin? To most, "Kremlin" means the seat of political power in Russia. For many centuries, this was where the country was run, from its early statehood in the Middle Ages to the decades of imperial and then superpower grandeur, excluding the two hundred years when St. Petersburg was the capital. In the international political parlance, "Kremlin" has become synonymous with the Soviet regime and its policy.

But the Kremlin was originally a fortress, a fortification to protect a town. Many other historical Russian cities, most notably Novgorod, Pskov, Kolomna, Smolensk and Nizhny Novgorod, have Kremlins of their own. Historians consider the Moscow Kremlin the largest historical fortress in Europe. And if you take into account its other historical specialisms as a royal palace, armory, treasury, royal burial vault, and occasionally also a prison, isn't it a bit like the Tower of London or the Spanish El Escorial?

But the Kremlin's image as a murky stronghold is outshined by the luster of its domes, and brightened by the cheerful chimes of the Ivan the Great bell tower. The Kremlin is also the religious nucleus of Russia, the stronghold of Russian Ortho-doxy, which is the persuasion of 80% of Russians. The Soviet government, which moved in after the 1917 Bolshevik Revolution, closed the Kremlin to the public. More than seven decades went by before religious life returned to the Kremlin's churches. But even today, much of the Kremlin remains a restricted area, and church services are not held regularly.

This Kremlin Guide, published by the National Geographic Society of Russia, will help you unravel all the mysteries and intricacies of the Kremlin. For centuries, the Kremlin and its adjacent Red Square have been viewed as an integral whole, so this guide also treats them as a single architectural complex, held sacred by every Russian. In popular lore and religious treaties alike, the Kremlin and Red Square were regarded as a sprawling outdoor temple, a piece of the Holy Land in Russia. In the past, when travelers entered the Kremlin through Red Square, the bond between the two was more clear. Now that they are separated it is more difficult to see, but this Guide will show you that it's still there.

Dmitry Grishin

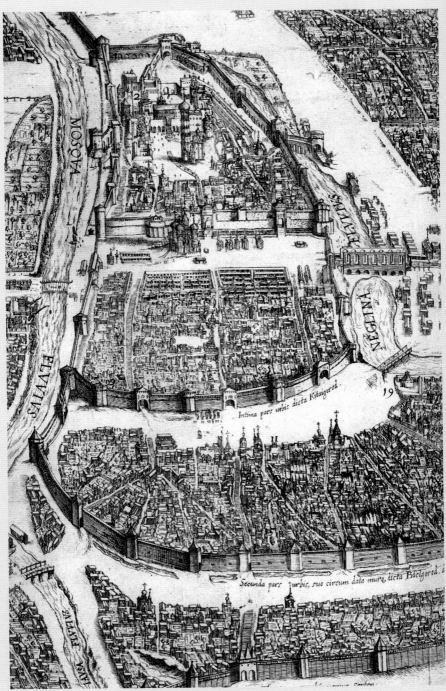

A fragment of the plan of Moscow, 1610

General Information

Thls guide provides a wealth of information, but also leaves a lot to one's imagination. You will find out what the Kremlin looked like centuries ago, what sacred objects and historic relics it holds and why they are significant.

Headpiece for the chapter Moscow from an old book, featuring some of the main symbols of Moscow: the Pushkin Monument, some revelers with an accordion, and the Kremlin

The guide will give you a glimpse of those Kremlin treasures and landmarks that are not on public display. Sneak a look at the hidden, cryptic and restricted part of the stronghold of the Russian government.

Now, before you walk into the Kremlin, let's answer some frequently asked questions.

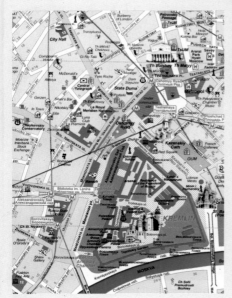

How to get to the Kremlin

Metro stations: Borovitskaya, Biblioteka im. Lenina, Aleksandrovsky Sad, Teatralnaya, Ploshchad Revolutsii, Okhotny Riad.

Borovitskaya and Biblioteka im. Lenina are the closest.

What to see inside the Kremlin

As you walk in through the Troitskie Gate, the building on your left is the Arsenal, a rare architectural landmark from the Peter the Great era. Next to the Arsenal stand some historical Russian cannons and trophy cannons from the 1812 Franco-Russian War. On your right, you can see the Poteshny Palace a little farther away, and the State Kremlin

View of the Kremlin in the 19th century

Palace at a closer distance. As you walk on, you get to the Czar Cannon and Czar Bell. At the opposite side of the square you can see the Senate building and the former ARCEC* Military School (currently an office building). You will be allowed to get closer to the Military School building if you follow pedestrian marks on the pavement. From here, you get a great view of the majestic Ivan the Great Bell Tower. From the Czar Bell, you will proceed to Cathedral Square with the Cathedrals of the Assumption, the Archangel Michael and the Annunciation, which are all open to general public along with the Church of the Deposition of the Robe, the Patriarch's Palace and Twelve Apostles' Church, and exhibits at the Single Pillar Room of the Patriarch's Palace, and at

---

The All-Russia Central Executive Committee – the supreme collective decision-making body in the Soviet Russia in the 1930's.

General Information

Arsenal

access controls and the unseen "red line" wherever you go inside the Kremlin. When you inadvertently cross that unseen line, you will be very audibly warned by Kremlin security guards. Please try to not bring any large objects or bags, otherwise you will be asked to leave them at the "left luggage" underneath the Kutafya Tower. If you carry some mace or another self-defense weapon, you will also be asked to leave it at the "left luggage".

the Ivan the Great Bell Tower. Visitors are also allowed on Palace Square in front of the main façade of the Grand Kremlin Palace.

Use the Borovitskie Gate to get to the Armory and the Diamond Depository.

Photos and videotaping

Visitors can take photos and videotape inside the Kremlin, but not inside the Armory or the museum churches.

Hours and tickets

The Kremlin is open daily, except Thursdays, from 10:00 am to 5:00 pm. The Armory admits tour groups at 10:00 am, 12:00 noon,

Poteshny (Fun) Palace

2:30 pm and 4:30 pm. Armory tickets are available one hour before the next scheduled admission. The ticket offices, located by the Kutafya Tower and in the Aleksandrovsky Garden, are open daily, except Thursdays, from 9:30 am to 4:00 pm. All tickets are valid on the day you bought them.

For service queries, booking a tour and exhibit information, please call the Kremlin's help desk at (495) 697-0349 from 9:00 am to 4:30 pm on weekdays. (This service is closed for lunch from 1:00 to 2:00 pm).

School and college students are entitled to discounts if they present their student ID.

Note that in your ticket, the Kremlin is referred to as "The National Museum and Preserve." (It is also the official residence of the President of Russia). It is, therefore, natural that the Kremlin is very heavily guarded. Hence the metal detectors, tight

Senat (on the left) and administrative building (on the right)

Additional services

The following additional services are available at the Kremlin museums:
– audio guided tours: 200 rub. at the ticket office No7, right of the Kutafya Tower.
– tours with a guide: general tickets (350 rub.) and 2500 rub. for the Kremlin territory

Ivan the Great Bell Tower

The Cathedral of the Assumption

and one of the cathedrals.

The Armory Tickets to the Armory are 700 rub. Tickets after student discount are 200 rub.

The Diamond Depository Ticket offices of the Diamond Depository are located in the premises of the exhibition. Use the Borovitskie Gate to get there. To get the tickets you should come to the ticket office by 10:00 am (except thirsday). Tickets are 500 rub. Ticket price after discount: 100 rub.

Architectural Landmarks At Cathedral Square

General tickets for all landmarks on Cathedral Square are 350 rub. Tickets after discount are 100 rub.

A general ticket covers all the architectural landmarks at Cathedral Square: five museum cathedrals, the Patriarch's Palace, exhibits at the Assumption Belfry or the Single Pillar Room of the Patriarch's Palace.

Exhibits at Single-Pillar Chamber of The Patriarch's Palace. Ticket price: 200 rub. Price after discount: 100 rub.

The Cathedral of the Archangel Michael

Guard Mounting Ceremony of The Presidential Regiment. From May to October, the Presidential Regiment holds displays of its Guard Mounting Ceremony on foot and on horseback at the Kremlin's Cathedral Square every Saturday at noon.

The last Saturday of each month, at 2:00 pm, the Presidential Regiment Guard Mounting Ceremony is held free for all in Red Square.

Cupolas of the Terem Palace churches and the Church of the Deposition of the Robe (on the right)

Restrooms

There are restrooms next to the ticket offices left of the Kutafya Tower, opposite the Visitor Information Center in the Aleksandrovsky Garden, at the souvenir shop near the Patriarch's Palace and at the Armory. There are also restrooms by the Kremlin wall at the entry to Red Square, near the Aleksandrovsky Garden.

Red Square

Entry to Red Square is free. The usual way to get to Red Square is from the north via the Voskresenskie Gate with Iverskaya Chapel (Metro stations: Ploshchad Revolutsii, Okhotny Riad and Teatralnaya).

Access to the Lenin Mausoleum and the tombs by the Kremlin wall is open from 10:00 am to 1:00 pm daily, except Mondays and Fridays. Visitors are not allowed to carry large objects or photographic or video equipment inside the Mausoleum. There is a left-luggage office at the corner of the History Museum.

The Cathedral of the Intercession

The Cathedral of the Intercession (St. Basil's Cathedral) is open from 11:00 am to 5:00 pm from november through april, and 11:00 am to 6:00 pm from may through oktober. The ticket offices close 20 minutes before temple closing time.

The Kremlin layout

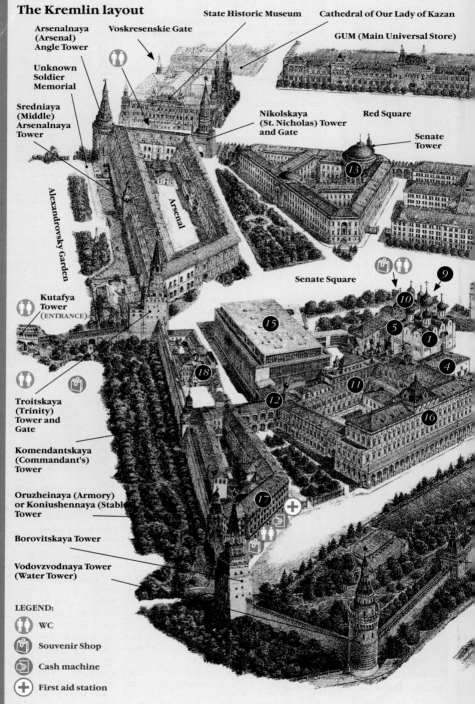

Arsenalnaya (Arsenal) Angle Tower

Unknown Soldier Memorial

Sredniaya (Middle) Arsenalnaya Tower

Alexandrovsky Garden

Arsenal

Voskresenskie Gate

State Historic Museum

Cathedral of Our Lady of Kazan

GUM (Main Universal Store)

Nikolskaya (St. Nicholas) Tower and Gate

Red Square

Senate Tower

Senate Square

Kutafya Tower (ENTRANCE)

Troitskaya (Trinity) Tower and Gate

Komendantskaya (Commandant's) Tower

Oruzheinaya (Armory) or Koniushennaya (Stable) Tower

Borovitskaya Tower

Vodovzvodnaya Tower (Water Tower)

LEGEND:

WC

Souvenir Shop

Cash machine

First aid station

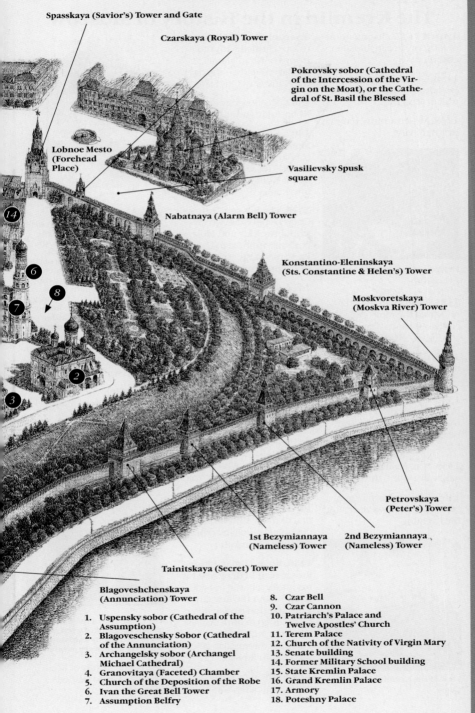

Spasskaya (Savior's) Tower and Gate

Czarskaya (Royal) Tower

Pokrovsky sobor (Cathedral of the Intercession of the Virgin on the Moat), or the Cathedral of St. Basil the Blessed

Lobnoe Mesto (Forehead Place)

Vasilievsky Spusk square

Nabatnaya (Alarm Bell) Tower

Konstantino-Eleninskaya (Sts. Constantine & Helen's) Tower

Moskvoretskaya (Moskva River) Tower

Petrovskaya (Peter's) Tower

1st Bezymiannaya (Nameless) Tower

2nd Bezymiannaya (Nameless) Tower

Tainitskaya (Secret) Tower

Blagoveshchenskaya (Annunciation) Tower

1. Uspensky sobor (Cathedral of the Assumption)
2. Blagoveschensky Sobor (Cathedral of the Annunciation)
3. Archangelsky sobor (Archangel Michael Cathedral)
4. Granovitaya (Faceted) Chamber
5. Church of the Deposition of the Robe
6. Ivan the Great Bell Tower
7. Assumption Belfry

8. Czar Bell
9. Czar Cannon
10. Patriarch's Palace and Twelve Apostles' Church
11. Terem Palace
12. Church of the Nativity of Virgin Mary
13. Senate building
14. Former Military School building
15. State Kremlin Palace
16. Grand Kremlin Palace
17. Armory
18. Poteshny Palace

The Kremlin in the History of Moscow

4 April 1147. First mention of Moscow in early Russian chronicles.

1156. Grand Prince Yuri Dolgoruky built a wooden wall in Moscow.

1238. Moscow burned down by Khan Batyi.

Defense of the Kremlin in the 13th century

1325. Metropolitan Peter relocated the Metropolis (religious capital) from Vladimir to Moscow.

1326. Ground broken for the first building of the Church of the Assumption.

1328. Ivan Kalita secured the powers of Grand Principality from the Tatar Khans, and became the principal collector of levies in Russia.

1339. Ivan Kalita built an oak wall around the Kremlin.

1365. Construction began on a white stone wall around the Kremlin.

View of the Kremlin in the 1370s

8 September 1380. Russian troops clashed with the troops of Khan Mamai at Kulikovo Field on the day of the Nativity of Our Lady.

1382. Moscow devastated by Khan Tokhtamysh.

1407. Khan Yedigei besieged Moscow but pulled back in exchange for a levy of 3,000 rubles. This was the last major Golden Horde foray into Russia.

1418. The Russian Orthodox Church split into two Metropolises: Kiev and Moscow, both subordinate to the Patriarch of the Universe in Constantinople.

1472. Grand Prince Ivan III married Sophia Paleolog the Princess of Byzantine. In this connection subsequently

Great Prince Ivan III, whose reign saw the existing Cathedral of the Assumption and the stone walls built in the Kremlin (1440–1505)

Russia adopted the Byzantine national emblem with a double eagle, which was then carved into the towers of the Kremlin.

1475–1479. A new Cathedral of the Assumption built, designed by Italian architect Aristotle Fioravanti.

1480. Khan Ahmat invaded Russia. Ivan III deployed his troops for a battle outside Moscow, but the Russian-Tatar standoff on the River Ugra ended in both armies withdrawing without a fight. The Tatar-Mongolian rule was over in Russia.

1480s. The new Cathedral of the Annunciation built.

In the 1460s, Ivan III first placed the image of a horseman defeating a dragon above the Kremlin's main entrance, the Frolus Gate. The image was copied from the emblem of the Kazan Khanate, with which Russia was at war. Before the early 18th century, the horseman had symbolized the Prince himself, then the Czar. In the 1710s, Peter I named the horseman "St. George" and ordered for it to be displayed on the emblem of Moscow

1485–1495. The existing Kremlin wall built.

1505–1509. The new Cathedral of the Archangel Michael built.

The Cathedral of the Archangel Michael looked even more cheerful early in its history, when its walls were painted red

1521. The troops of Khan Magmet-Girei invaded Moscow.

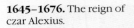

History

According to legend, the miraculous assistance of the Icon of Our Lady of Vladimir was instrumental in helping Moscow fight off its enemies in 1395, 1480 and 1521

1534–1538. Kitai-Gorod wall built during the reign of Ivan the Terrible's mother, Grand Princess Elena Glinskaya.

1547–1584. The reign of the first Russian Czar, Ivan IV (Ivan the Terrible, who ruled from 1533 on, but first as a Grand Prince).

1549. The first Land Assembly convened by Ivan the Terrible in Moscow.

1554–1560. The St. Basil's Cathedral built in Red Square to commemorate the conquest of Kazan.

19 April 1564. The first book printed in Moscow, titled The Apostle.

1571. Moscow devastated by the Crimean Khan Devlet-Girei. Only the Kremlin survived the fire.

1591. Crimean Khan Kazy-Girei invaded.

1598. Czar Theodore died, ending the Rurik Dynasty that had ruled Russia for seven centuries. A Land Assembly named Boris Godunov the first elected Czar of Russia.

April 1605. Boris Godunov died (deposed in May 1606), and the period known as "Time of Troubles" aggravated (until 1612). Dmitry the Impostor usurped the throne in Moscow.

1610–1612. Moscow invaded by Polish troops.

4 November 1612. Moscow freed by a home guard force led by Minin and Pozharsky.

February 1613. Mikhail Romanov constituted as Czar by the Land Assembly, starting the rule of the Romanov Family.

1625. A multilevel top with chiming clock added to the Kremlin's Spasskaya (Savior's) Tower.

1645–1676. The reign of czar Alexius.

1653. Unification of Ukraine and Russia, proposed by the Ukrainian Rada in Pereyaslavl, ratified by the Land Assembly, convened at the Kremlin's Granovitaya Chamber.

Czar Mikhail entering Moscow in 1613

1670–1680s. The Kremlin towers built up to their present height and look.

May 1682. Strelets Guard troops rebelled in the Kremlin. John and Peter both declared Czars, and Sophia declared Ruler. The "Tripartite Rule" continued until 1689.

1689–1725. The reign of Peter I the Great.

1698. The last Strelets mutiny suppressed. Strelets guards executed in Red Square, and the Strelets troop disbanded.

1700. Peter I decreed for Russia to switch to Western calendar, counting its years from the Birth of Our Lord instead of the Creation, as before (the difference was 5508 years). Russia celebrated its first New Year's Eve with the rest of Europe in winter with fireworks in Red Square.

October 1700. Patriarch Adrian died. The institution of Patriarchy abolished.

Prince Dmitry Pozharsky and Kuzma Minin in 1612

Peter the Great

1701. Peter I decreed for Russia's first public theater to be set up in Red Square.

1703. The first Russian newspaper — Vedomosti — printed in Moscow.

1703. Peter I declared public display of poverty a felony in Moscow. Beggars removed from their traditional spots in the Kremlin and outside St. Basil's Cathedral.

1712. St. Petersburg declared the capital of Russia instead of Moscow.

1710s. Peter I decided to call the horseman displayed on Moscow's official seals "St.

The young Emperor Peter II died in Moscow in 1730, ending the male line of the ruling Romanov Family. He was the last Romanov buried at the Cathedral of the Archangel Michael

George", and ordered the same image to be made the emblem of Moscow.

1721. Peter I constituted the Synod as the supreme religious authority of the Russian Orthodox Church with the title "The Holiest," which had previously been awarded only to Patriarchs. The Synod would rule until 1917–1918, when Patriarchy was re-instituted in Russia.

1755. Russia's first university founded in Moscow (initially housed in the Land Office building, where the History Museum now stands in Red Square).

1786. Lobnoe Mesto set up in Red Square in its present shape.

1776–1787. The Kremlin's Senate built, now the main residence of the President of Russia.

1804. Red Square received its first cobblestone pavement.

September 1812. Napoleon's troops invaded the Kremlin. Fires began to sweep Moscow.

11 October 1812. Napoleon left Moscow after attempting to blow up the Kremlin. The majority of churches and towers survived.

1813–1826. The Kremlin renovated.

21 February 1818. Monument to Minin and Pozharsky unveiled in Red Square.

17 April 1818. Future Emperor Alexander II born in the Kremlin's Nicholas's Small Palace (Alexander II is a national hero in Finland, and there is a monument in his honor in Helsinki).

1838–1849. The Grand Kremlin Palace built.

1844–1851. The Kremlin Armory built in its present shape.

The Nicholas's Small Palace was demolished in 1929

5 March 1861. On Forgiving Sunday (the Sunday before the Lent), Emperor Alexander II's Manifesto on the Abolition of Serfdom in Russia was read out in the Cathedral of the Assumption (the same day, the Manifesto was read out loud in all the churches of Moscow and St. Petersburg).

27 May 1883. The Alexander III Museum of History opened in Red Square.

1893. Europe's largest shopping center – Verkhnie Torgovye Riady (now G.U.M.) – opened in Red Square.

The view of the Monument to Minin and Pozharsky in the middle of the 19th century

14 May 1896. Nicholas II, the last Emperor of Russia, crowned in the Kremlin's Cathedral of the Assumption.

1898. Alexander II monument unveiled in the Kremlin (later demolished by the Bolsheviks).

1912. The 100th anniversary of Russia's 1812 victory over Napoleon celebrated. Alexander III monument unveiled in the plaza in front of the Church of Christ the Savior in Moscow. The Alexander III Museum of Fine Arts opened next to the church in Moscow's Volkhonka neighborhood (now Pushkin Art Museum).

The monument to Alexander II was demolished after the October Socialist revolution

1913. Nationwide celebration of the 300th anniversary of the Romanov rule. An obelisk built in the Alexandrovsky Garden.

August 1914. The Emperor's Declaration of War on Germany read out at Lobnoe Mesto in Red Square.

2 March 1917. Nicholas II abdicated.

October – November 1917. The National Church Assembly, convened in the Kremlin, ruled to reestablish the institution of Patriarchy in Russia.

March 1918. Moscow made the capital once again. The Soviet government moved into the Kremlin, which was from then on closed to general public. All services stopped at Kremlin churches.

1922. Valuables requisitioned from the Kremlin's churches, ostensibly as famine relief. Around 1 ton of gold and silver removed from the Assumption Cathedral alone.

1929. The Chudov (Holy Miracle) and Voznesensky (Ascension) Monasteries demolished in the Kremlin.

5 December 1931. The Church of Christ the Savior demolished (blown up). The oldest Kremlin church — the Church of the Icon of Our Savior of Bor — also demolished.

November 1935. The double eagles on the Kremlin towers replaced with pentagonal stars.

24 June 1945. WWII Victory Parade held in Red Square.

1961. The Palace of Congresses opened in the Kremlin.

1988. 1000th anniversary of Russia's conversion to Christianity celebrated. A number of churches returned to religious authorities in Moscow.

October 1989. The Cathedral of the Assumption hosted its first sermon after a more than 70-year interruption.

December 1991. Mikhail Gorbachev, the first and last elected President of the Soviet Union, resigned. The red flag lowered above the Kremlin, and the pre-1917 Russian tricolor flag raised.

November 1993. Russia's historical national emblem — the double eagle — restored.

7 May 2000 and **7 May 2004.** Vladimir Putin was inaugurated as President of

During the Soviet era, May 1 was transformed into a secular International Workers' Solidarity Day, celebrated with pompous and colorful parades in Red Square that had replaced the traditional Palm Sunday and Easter festivities

Russia for his first and second term with a ceremony held at the St. Andrew Hall of the Grand Kremlin Palace, where the Russian National Flag, the President's Flag, the Russian Constitution, and the Presidential Order for Outstanding Service to the Homeland 1st Class were featured as symbols of presidential power. After the ceremony, the President proceeded to the Church of the Annunciation to be blessed by Alexius II, the Orthodox Patriarch of Moscow and All Russia.

10 March 2006. The Moscow Kremlin museums marked their 200th anniversary.

Since 1994 the new State Emblem – double eagle – replaced the Emblem of the USSR on the wall of the State Kremlin Palace

Uspensky sobor
(Cathedral of the Assumption)

Located to the northen side of Sobornaya Ploschad (Cathedral Square), the Cathedral of the Assumption was the main church of the Russian state for the period of 500 years.

It was here that Prince Dmitry Donskoy prayed before going into battle with Mamai, and Czar Alexius, before leaving for the war with Poland, and Peter the Great before his campaigns against the Swedes and the Turks. In July 1812, after the French invasion, Emperor Alexander I, having reverently visited the relics of the Moscow saints, swore an oath to continue the war with Napoleon.

Until end of the 19th century imperial weddings and coronations were held here. Following the coronation, representatives from all classes swore an oath of loyalty to the sovereign. It was in this cathedral that the metropolitans and patriarchs of the All-Russian Orthodox Church were invested with their duties.

The cathedral was founded in 1326 under Prince Ivan Kalita by the holy Metropolitan Peter and dedicated in honour of the Assumption of the Virgin, following the example of the main church of the ancient monastery in Kievan-Rus, Pecherskaya Lavra (11th century). Uspenie (from which the word Uspensky is derived, meaning "assumption") means "blessed death". Metropolitan Peter himself decided on the location in the future cathedral, where he was later buried, and, according to legend, cut out a stone coffin for himself. He died several months

◄—— **On 13 October 1989, Patriarch Pimen was the first Patriarch after a seventy year break to hold a service on the day of All Russian Saints.**

after he had consecrated the foundation of the church and bequeathed all his personal belongings to its construction.

A crypt is now located in the church with ten Moscow metropolitans and nine patriarchs. The burial places themselves are located beneath the floor of the cathedral, and above them are located their headstones.

The cathedral is usually open the same hours as the other museums of the Kremlin. Religious services are carried out on important religious holidays, saint days of those saints buried here and on a few other days with the participation of the Most Holy Patriarch. Entrance is gained by invitation of the Moscow Patriarchy. On the days of St. Cyril and St. Methodius, apostles for the Slavic peoples (24 May), a religious celebration is held from the cathedral through Spasskie (Saviour's) Gate to Slavyanskaya (Slavic) Square.

"Like a solid rock" wrote a chronicler, describing the harmonious, majestic look of the Cathedral of the Assumption

The External View

The majestic cathedral is built to a square plan. The height including the cross on the top is 45 metres. The walls are built from white stone and the arches and remaining parts of the building are made from brick, which was manufactured by the Andronevsky Monastery on the Yauza river where brickworks were especially established. The arch is supported by 4 columns with a thickness greater than two metres.

The builder of the cathedral, Aristotel Fioravanti was invited from Italy by Ivan III after the previous building, built by Russian masters Ivan Krivtsov and Mishkin, had col-

Layout of the Cathedral

One of the great relics — a Nail of the Lord formerly housed in the side altar of Peter and Paul

Beneath the north-eastern cupola is the side altar named after the apostles Peter and Paul. Each Prince swore loyalty to the Great Prince in this chapel

One of the best frescoes of the old altar barrier — the image of st. Alexius, Man of God

In the place the Icon of the Holy Virgin of Vladimir was displayed, a copy is now displayed

Decorative frieze

By the corner of the northern wall is a cross, which marks the burial place of Metropolitan Iona (†1461). His shrine is located inside the cathedral

Main entrance

Canopy which now houses a shrine with the relics of Patriarch Germogen

Frescoes on the eastern wall. In the semi circular arch parallel to the central image of the Holy Trinity are depictions of the Holy Wisdom as a fiery angel and the Praise for the Holy Virgin — the adoration of Maria with her child

Beneath the south-eastern cupola is the side altar of Praise of the Holy Virgin, built in 1452 by Metropolitan Iona in memory of the deliverance of Moscow from Tartar invasion. The metropolitans and patriarchs were defrocked here until the 17th century

In the decorative frieze there are depictions of Moscow and Novgorod Saints

The Patriarch's prayer seat

The Monomakh Throne (Czar's prayer seat)

A detail from the carvings on the Monomakh Throne

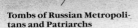

Tombs of Russian Metropolitans and Patriarchs

Prayer seat for Russian Czarina and princesses

Uspensky Sobor

Above the southern entrance to the Cathedral is a depiction of the Mother of Christ with archangels Gabriel and Michael

lapsed. The exact cause of the destruction of the building has never been established — it is possible that it was caused by a small earthquake, or possibly the lime used in the construction of the church was not of high enough quality. The construction of the cathedral lasted four short years.

The external frescoes probably appeared immediately after the construction was completed and later renewed. Above the southern entrance to the Cathedral, which was the main one in antiquity, is a Vladimirsky depiction of the Virgin with the archangels Micheal and Gabriel. Beneath, in a decorative frieze are saints from the Russian Church. Above the portal there is the image The Divine Saviour, and Archangel Michael and a guardian angel protect the entrance.

The internal doors of the southern entrance are known as the Korsunskie (since according to legend they were brought from the city of Korsun) or the Golden Gate — covered with ten bronze sheets, which have biblical scenes, patterns and inscriptions written in Old Slavonic. In the upper part of the gate there are depictions taken from events in biblical history, and beneath are Ancient Greek philosophers (Plato, Aristotle, etc.) and pagan prophetesses — the Sybils, foretelling the birth of Jesus Christ.

Above the northern entrance are depictions of Russian saints. Higher up is located a deesis, the image of Christ, the Virgin and John the Baptist with a gathering of the Apostles and St. Nicholas the Miracle Worker. The entrance is also guarded by Archangel Michael and a guardian angel.

On the eastern wall in the corner there are also frescoes. In the centre of the image is the Holy Trinity: sitting on the throne is the God the Father and the Son of God and between them the Holy Spirit is represented as a dove. To the right is the Holy Wisdom, seen as a fiery angel and the Virgin Mary winged, with St. John the Baptist. To the left is the Praise for the Virgin, worshiping Mary with her child, which symbolises the presence in the church of a side altar of the same dedication.

Internal Frescoes

The entrance to the cathedral nowadays is through the western atrium. It was formerly used during coronations, religious and other processions. "Privileged" beggars also sat here (each of the Kremlin Cathedrals had such beggars). The present day view of the cathedral with the enclosed vestibules and oak doors and the atrium dates from the 19th century. From the frescoes, only the scene of the apocalypse survives on the arches of the atrium.

On entering the cathedral produces an indelible impression. It is illuminated by an enormous chandelier. Since originally there was no electricity. As in all of the Kremlin churches, only candles made from pure bee wax were used. In contrast to paraffin candles, they did not flicker, creating a soft

In the cathedral's frescoes there are 249 scenes and 2066 individual figures

light, warmth and a particularly fragrant smell. The central chandelier, shaped like a giant head of wheat weighs approximately 330 kg and was cast from silver, seized from Napoleon's troops by the Cossack forces of Ataman Platov (the master was the Swedish silver smith Gedling).

Heating was installed in 1856 before the coronation of Emperor Alexander II. Previously, in several winters it had been necessary to attend the services in temperatures as low as −10 to −13 degrees centigrade.

The cathedral was decorated in 1513–15 by order of Great Prince

A picture between the columns on the arches of the cathedral

Vasily III. After 150 years the paint had lost its richness and in 1642–1643 Czar Mikhail Romanov gave orders for it to be redecorated. A fine layer of gold was applied over the original paintings. Almost 500 square metres were covered with this layer, and all the former frescoes were replicated on it. One hundred and fifty icon painters from different cities throughout Russia participated in this work.

The present frescoes mainly date from the time of Mikhail Romanov, with several fragments dating to the end of the 15th — early 16th century. In it are depicted 249 scenes and 2066 individual figures.

Under the main cupola is a depiction of Almighty Christ. Under the other four cupolas there is the Saviour Emmanuel (beyond the iconostasis, Christ as a Young Boy), The Lord Saboath (God the Father), The Divine Saviour and the image of the Virgin of the Sign. On the arches are frescoes on the theme of the Twelve Great Feasts of the Orthodox Christian year.

On the walls there are depictions of events from the Gospel and the seven Ecumenical Councils, which confirmed the doctrine of the Orthodox faith. On the southern and northern walls are events from the life of the Holy Mother of Christ and scenes of her glorification.

On the four pillars, supporting the vaults of the church, are depictions of martyrs, (in all over 140). They are "the pillars and confirmation of the faith" according to church doctrine. Above the southern doors there are images of St. Helena, discovering the Lord's Cross on Golgotha, and the Emperor Constantine, the founder of Constantinople, and above the northern doors, comparable to the other two in significance, St. Olga, the first Christian princess of the Rus and St. Vladimir. On the eastern wall, which is hidden from view behind the altar are depictions of the Patriarchy and saints of the Greek and Russian Church.

Almost all of the western side, as is tradition, is covered with an image of the Day of Judgement. A pilgrim, leaving the church, would remember the terrifying pictures of hellish suffering and shun earthly temptations. According to those times, it depicts the unbelievers in the nether world in western clothes and white frill.

Historical Relics

By the columns opposite the iconostasis are located three objects of interest: The Monomakh Throne (the czar's seat for prayer), the Patriarch's prayer area and the Princess's prayer seat.

The Monomakh Throne (czar's prayer seat)

Uspensky Sobor

The Patriarch's prayer seat is a stone tabernacle, upholstered with crimson velvet

The Monomakh Throne was placed in the cathedral by the first Russian Czar, Ivan the Terrible in 1551, several years after he was crowned. The wood is now blackened with age. The throne is named "Monomakh" because it has depicted on it scenes from the life of Prince Vladimir Monomakh. One of the scenes (on the backside of the throne near the wall) shows how Vladimir Monomakh received his famous Monomakh Hat and other symbols of royal power from Byzantium from his grandfather, Emperor Constantine. The supports for the throne were made in the shape of four animals. According to the historian Ivan Zabelin, they represent a lion, hyena, and two nameless predators.

This throne was the symbol of the Grand Principality of the Rus. Emperor Peter the Great also added

On the apex of the pavilion of the throne on three sides there are scenes from the birth of the Virgin, Christ and St. John the Baptist, prayer symbols for the continuation of the dynasty

to its significance. He gave orders that it should remain in the cathedral after Russia was declared an empire, and coronations were performed in the European manner. The future empress, Catherine I, sat on the Monomakh Throne while Peter the Great placed the new crown on her. From that time onwards all Russian empresses right up to Catherine II symbolically ascended the Monomakh Throne. Under Pavel I this tradition came to an end.

By the south-western column is located the Patriarch's prayer seat. It is stone, padded with crimson velvet. The metropolitans and patriarchs prayed here, when they themselves were not performing the divine service. In this seat in 1568 Metropolitan St. Filipp publicly refused to bless Ivan the Terrible and denounced him for his lawlessness.

By the north east column is the Czarina's prayer seat, where the princesses were during the service. On the apex of the pavilion of the throne on three sides there are scenes from the birth of the Virgin, Christ and St. John the Baptist, prayer symbols for the continuation of the dynasty. On the upholstery of the internal walls hangs the National Emblem of the Russia Sovereign State — the double headed eagle, on its wings are the coats of arms of Russian cities and on its breast, George the Victorious, the symbol for Moscow framed by the chains of the Order of St. Andrew the First Called (the highest honour in Russia).

By the western wall of the cathedral, of the entrance, to the right of the entrance stands a bronze tabernacle with a delicate lattice in which is located a shrine with the relics of Patriarch Germogen. This tabernacle (formerly known as a canopy, is sometimes called Sverchkov's Tabernacle) was poured in 1624 by Dmitry Sverchkov by the wishes of Patriarch Filaret for preserving the Lord's Tomb. The following year a part of the robe of Christ, sent to Moscow by Shah Abbas of Persia as a gift, was deposited in the tabernacle. The relic came to the Shah during the capture of Georgia where it had been preserved in local cathedral there. The canopy was an imitation of the cave, which served as the tomb of the Lord in Jerusalem, and inside, in accordance with this symbolism a

The Czarina's prayer seat was arranged in the 17ᵗʰ century

coffin was made from sanctified cypress wood. The fate of the Lord's Coffin is now unknown and the current sepulchre of Patriarch Germogen lies beneath the shrine, made from bronze in 1913.

Icons

On most days the cathedral possesses the feel of a museum. The images in the iconostasis are missing their frames, several have been taken and in their place frescoes of the old altar barrier of the 15ᵗʰ century (discovered in 1882) are visible. Other icons are housed in glass and are displayed before the iconostasis thematically, contrary to what was done traditionally in churches. Those who have participated in the religious services here say that during the services this museum atmosphere markedly changes and the ancient magnificence of the cathedral is unveiled.

The iconostasis consists of five rows, rising up almost to the vaulted ceiling, built in 1652–1653. It reflects the idea of unity between the Old and New Testaments. On the highest row, icons of the Patriarchs were traditionally located, in the centre — Lord God Saboath. In the second row were placed the prophets of the Old Testament with the icon of the Mother of Christ of the Sign in the middle. In the third row, and smaller, were located icons with the themes of religious celebrations and evangelical events — Twelve Great Feasts. The fourth row (Deisis) symbolizes the New Testament with the Savior as a bishop on the throne in the centre, and to his left and right sides, the Holy Virgin, John the Baptist and the Apostles.

The relics, displayed in the lowest row (sometimes called Sovereign) were collected by Moscow princes down the centuries from different cities and principalities united to Moscow — Vladimir, Smolensk, Novgorod, Pskov and Ustug.

The Miraculous Icon of Our Lady of Vladimir, the most honoured of all the Kremlin relics, was located to the left of the Holy Doors in a separate case and was encased with diamonds and gold. Now, the ancient image is kept in the Church of St. Nicholas in Tolmachi, near Tretyakov Gallery, and in its place, in a gilded case (1883) there is a copy dating from the 16ᵗʰ century.

You will not find a more significant icon in Russia, even given the richness of Russian iconography. Church tradition tells that the icon was painted by the evangelist St. Luka during the lifetime of the Holy Virgin, who highly praised the painting and said that the place where it lay would be protected and receive her patronage.

Cathedral's icon of the Assumption of the Virgin

A fragment of the icon of Our Lady of Vladimir

Image of the Allmighty Savior, or The Savior of the Fiery Eye

However, specialists date the icon as coming from the 12th century, although it is possible to suggest that it is a copy of the original. The tradition about the origin of the icon came about, evidently, towards the end of the 15th century, after the Rus had dealt with several foreign invasions and occupiers, who had captured among other things the miraculous icon.

In Uspensky Sobor there are also copies of the Vladimir Icon, which have come to be as highly revered, as the original image. The frame of the original miracle working icon and two of its copies are now located in the Armory.

The icon of The All Merciful Savior on the Throne, which is revered for its miraculous qualities is located to the right of the Holy Doors, where it was placed in 1655 by the will of Patriarch Nikon. The icon is painted a board dating to the 11th century.

To the right of The Saviour is the church's icon of the Assumption of the

Northern side of the Cathedral

1. The Icon of Mother of Christ of Tikhvin with 103 stamp images (17th century).
2. Icon of the Holy Virgin with scenes of life of Zosima and Savvaty Solovetsky (16th century). Brought from the Solovetsky Monastery after its closure in the 1920s.
3. St. Alexander of Svir (c. 1547).
4. St. Nicholas, one of older icons (dating to the beginning of the 15th century).
5. Icon of Our Lady of Bogolyubovo (16th century)

and other images from the 16th–17th centuries, including a copy of the Icon of Our Lady of Vladimir.
6. St. Sergei Radonezhsky (late 15th – early 16th century). Beneath the icon is the image of Alexius, Man of God, and Mary of Egypt — the patron saints of Czar Alexius and his first wife Maria (17th century).
7. Display window with icons which are frequently changed in order to display the full treasury of relics from the Kremlin museums.

Uspensky Sobor

Virgin. Specialists believe that this icon dates back to the 15th century and it is likely that the image was painted specially for the new cathedral. In the icon, beyond the Virgin is Christ who is caring a child, which represents Mary's soul.

Near the image of the Assumption, there is a picture of The Saviour on the Throne (14th–15th century).

On the left side from the Holy Doors, an ancient altar barrier with frescoes dating to the time of Ivan III was uncovered

Above the southern doors of the iconostasis is a copy of the Icon of Our Lady of Tikhvin, which is considered to be blessed with miraculous properties. Under the pledge of this icon the Treaty of Stolbovo was signed with Sweden in 1617.

Nearby is located another ancient icon in which Christ is depicted in the vestments of a bishop, which is reminiscent of the dress of the Byzantine emperors, and the Mother of Christ is dressed in the imperial clothes of a queen with a golden crown. It is probable that the image was painted in the 14th century by a Serbian master.

Above the door, leading to the side altar of Dimitry Solunsky, is an image of the Almighty Saviour the Fiery Eye (14th century).

To the left from the Holy Doors, after the Icon of Our Lady of Vladimir, at the end of the 19th century an ancient altar barrier was uncovered with frescoes dating to the time of Ivan III and this was left for viewing. These frescoes were carried out in the 1480s by icon painters from Dionisy's artisan group.

In the case by the northern wall of the cathedral is located an icon from the 12th century with the image of St. George. The

Southern side of the cathedral

1. Apocalypse or the Revelation of John the Evangelist.
2. Metropolitan Peter with stamp images, it is suggested that it is the work of Dionisy.
3. She Rejoices in You named after the first words of a hymn in reverence of the Holy Virgin.
4. Solovetsky Monastery with the miracle workers Zosima and Savvaty.
5. Praise for the Virgin, 14th century, Novgorod. One of the oldest icons in Rus with such a theme.

6. The Icon of Our Lady of Jerusalem.
7. Display window with icons which are frequently changed in order to display the full treasury of relics from the Kremlin museums. Among the revered icons in the display window is the Golden Haired Savior, so named since the hair of the Savior really was painted with gold, which symbolizes His Divine light (13th century).
8. Monomakh Throne of Ivan the Terrible, the Czar's Prayer Seat.

The Icon of Our Lady of Vladimir is revered for its miraculous properties. The Holy Virgin is thought of as the patron of Russia. Original icon is now located in the St. Nicholas's Church in Tolmachi, nearby the Tretyakov Gallery

picture of the saint was unexpectedly discovered beneath oil paints on the reverse side of an icon of the Virgin during restoration work in the 1930s. The saint is depicted, not as he usually is upon a horse, but with the defeated snake waist high. The Russian people revered St. George as the helper of farmers and warriors, guardian of livestock and on the whole, as developer of Russian territory.

In other cases before the iconostasis are housed: the icon of Crucifixion from the 15th century and the icon of the Holy Virgin of Korsun, the work of 13th century Byzantine masters. On the Crucifixion is a Greek inscription "You have been summoned and you have been reviled...O Savior, suffer and die for the sake of mortal man...".

In cases by the western wall near the "replacement" copy of the Icon of Our Lady of Vladimir, is an icon from the 16th century, a Moscow piece, Crucifixion with scenes from the New Testament and

The Lord's Nail and the cover of its shrine made from precious stone where it is kept

the image of the Saviour — one of the first works by Moscow icon painters (the first half of the 14th century).

In the enclosed area of the northern and southern walls there are displays of various venerated smaller icons. The bigger icons are displayed in the bronze iconostasis on the walls.

Holy Relics

Formerly, holy relics were stored in the cathedral which were then transferred to collections in the Kremlin museums. In the 18th century in the church there were: part of the Robe of Christ, part of the Robe of the Holy

An open canopy, in which the shrine with the relics of Patriarch Germogen are kept

Virgin (both of them known in historical sources from the 5th century onwards), a nail of the Lord. The part of the Robe of Christ was brought to Moscow in 1625, and were divided, one part was kept at the cathedral while another was continually taken home by Muscovites to help them carry out their prayers.

The part of the Robe of the Holy Mother was brought to Uspensky Cathedral as a gift by Prince Vasily Golytsyn after his Crimean campaign.

The Nail of the Lord — this is one of the four nails which, according to tradition was used at Calvary to crucify Christ. According to tradition the Nail of the Lord was sent by Emperor Constantine to the Georgian Czar, having converted to Christianity and was preserved by the Georgian Czars. In 1686 Czar Archil, returning to Moscow took it with him. By order of Peter the Great, the relic was transferred to Uspensky Sobor along with the gold shrine.

Here also other great relics were kept: a hand of the apostle Andrew the First Called, part of the relics of John the Baptist, the head of St. Grigory the Scholar, the head of St. John, bishop os Constantinople, and relics of Russian saints.

The Altar of St. Peter and St. Paul

In this area (behind the iconostasis from the northern side) each prince kissed the cross as a sign of loyalty to the Great Prince of Moscow. It was here also, until the establishment of the patriarchy in the 16th century that the metropolitan received his office.

The shrine of the metropolitan St. Peter, the cathedral's founder, is located to the left of the altar, between the altar of St. Peter and the main altar, and you can see it when the Northern Gate of iconostasis is open.

In the altar of St. Peter and Paul there was a rare stone coloured icon of George the Victorious

In the side chapel of St. Peter and Paul are located particular shrines for the relics of famous Orthodox saints. In the section there was a rare Vlakhernskaya Icon of the Holy Virgin, the patron of the Byzantine emperors. Now it is exhibited in a glass case by the northern wall of the cathedral. The icon was executed using an unusual method with wax. In 1654 it was sent as a gift to Czar Alexius Romanov from the Patriarchy in Constantinople.

The Altar of Praise of the Holy Virgin

Even in the time of Prince Ivan Kalita, the Metropolitan Iona built a side altar of Praise of the Holy Virgin in thanks for her help during the battle between Ivan III and Khan Akhmat. It is particularly interesting to note that the Feast of Praise of the Holy Virgin is celebrated on Saturday of the fifth week of Lent and in 1147 this was April 5. And it was on that day that Prince Yury Dolgoruky, the founder of Moscow, dined with his allies and this was the reason that the area of Moscow was first noted in the chronicles.

The Altar of Dimitry Solunsky

Located behind the iconostasis from the southern side. It is possible that on this place is the oldest burial site in Moscow, the burial place of Prince Yury, the brother of Ivan Kalita (†1325), although the headstone has not been preserved. Yury, having given his loyalty to the Golden Horde, married the sister of Uzbek Khan and was the first Moscow prince to receive the title of Great Prince. In this very section in 1547 Yury Glinsky (the uncle of Ivan the Terrible) hid himself from an enraged mob, but was captured

and killed. He was accused of witchcraft and burning Moscow.

Sepulchres and Shrines of the Moscow Saints

Many Moscow metropolitans and all patriarchs, apart from the disgraced patriarch Nikon (1652–1658), were buried here. He, as is famous, was removed from his position and was buried in Novy Ierusalim (New Jerusalem) near Moscow. The relics of the metropolitan St. Alexius (†1378) also lie here: initially they were kept at Chudov (Miracle) Monastery, but now in Bogoyavlensky Sobor in Moscow. If you detour around the shrines from left to right, in a clockwise direction, then you will go in chronological order of the saints, except for the most revered which can be found at the altar and by the corners of the cathedral.

The first, in the north-western corner, to the left from the entrance, is the shrine with relics to Metropolitan, St Jonah (1448–1461). He was the first bishop to be chosen without the participation of the Constantinople

The shrine of Metropolitan, St. Peter

The relics of St. Peter, the founder of Uspensky Sobor are kept in a silver shrine at the altar of St. Peter and Paul

This sumptuously decorated, unusually large 17ᵗʰ century Gospel from the sacristy of the Cathedral of the Assumption was a gift from Czarina Natalia, second wife of czar Alexius. Currently stored in the Armory

The iconostasis of the altar of Dimitry Solunsky

Sacristy

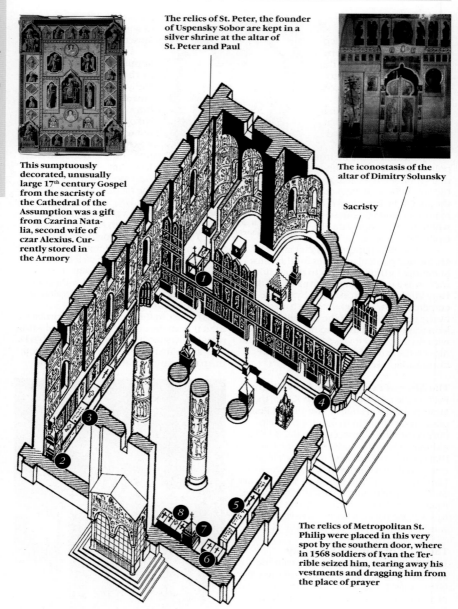

The relics of Metropolitan St. Philip were placed in this very spot by the southern door, where in 1568 soldiers of Ivan the Terrible seized him, tearing away his vestments and dragging him from the place of prayer

1. Shrine of Metropolitan St. Peter (†1326) and tomb of Metropolitan Feognost (†1353).
2. Shrine of Metropolitan Jonah (†1461).
3. The tomb of metropolitans Geronty, (†1489), Simon (†1511), St. Makary (†1563) and Philip I (†1473).

4. Shrine of Metropolitan Philip II (†1570).
5. Tombes of patriarchs Iosif (†1652), St. Iov (†1607), Ioasaf I (†1642) and Philaret (†1633).
6. The tombs of metropolitans Kiprian (†1406) and Foty (†1431).
7. The canopy where the shrine of Patriarch St. Germogen is located (†1612).
8. The tombs of patriarchs Ioasaf II (†1672), Pitirim (†1673), Ioakim (†1690) Adrian (†1700).

Shrine of Metropolitan St. Iona, constructed by Czar Feodor

Patriarchy (from that point onwards the Russian church became independent).

Further on, by the northern wall is the burial area for metropolitans from the 15th–16th centuries: Geronty (1473–1489), Simon (1496–1511), Makary (1542–1563). Metropolitan Makary was famous as the author of a large work on the lives of the saints and in this way enabled the glorification of many Russian saints. In 1547 Makary crowned the 17 year old Ivan the Terrible and had a positive influence in the first years of his reign. The next tomb after Makary's has written on it that Metropolitan Afanasy is buried here. However, it is believed that the inscription is incorrect and Metropolitan Philip I (1464–1473) is buried there instead.

At the right end of the iconostasis, near the southern doors, is located the shrine with relics of metropolitan, Saint Philip II (1566–1568), who raised his voice against

Patriarch Filaret. (Feodor Romanov), the father of the first czar of the Romanov Dynasty — Mikhail (†1633)

the lawless actions of Ivan the Terrible and was later throttled by the order of the Czar. It was here in 1568 that the metropolitan was seized by soldiers of the Czar and dragged him from the cathedral tearing off his vestments.

Further along the southern and western walls are buried nine patriarchs: Iosif (1642–1652), St. Iov — the first Moscow Patriarch of all Rus (1589–1605), Ioasaf I (1634–1642), Philaret (1619–1633), St. Germogen (1606–1612), Ioasaf II (1667–1672), Pitirim (1672–1673), Ioakim (1674–1690) and, finally, Adrian, (1690–1700). Between them in the south west corner is located two early tombs (15th century) — locally revered saints the metropolitans Kiprian (1378–1406) and Foty (1409–1431).

Patriarch Philaret (the furthest tomb by the southern wall), was the father of the first Czar of the Romanov Dynasty. He was forced to become a monk by Boris Godunov suspecting him of conspiracy.

The coronation of Alexander II in the Cathedral of the Assumption on 26 August 1856

Cathedral of the Assumption: Ascending the Throne

During four hundred years, from the end of the 15th through the end of the 19th century, the Cathedral of the Assumption was the venue of the most important ritual in Russia — the crowning later known as coronation (as is well known, from the Latin word corona meaning a "crown"). This ritual was performed in the Cathedral 21 times. However, not all who were crowned occupied the throne and not all of those crowned were real czars.

The first to be crowned there was Dmitry, on 4 February 1498, a grandson of Ivan III, and the last was Emperor Nicholas II and Empress Alexandra whose joint coronation took place on 14 May 1896. The paradox is that having attained the absolute power on earth they ended their lives in prison.

The first crowning ceremony in the Cathedral of the Assumption in 1498. Great Prince Ivan III places the crown on his grandson Dmitry

Ancient Russia — Moscovite Principality

The ritual of the coronation came to Russia from Byzantium, and the Byzantines adopted it from the ancient Israelites. Before that the Russian princes had followed a ritual of enthronement of which we have little knowledge. We can only assume that it was a kind of a princely ancestral throne placed in the church. The prince who inherited the throne from his kinsman secured the blessing of a priest, ascended the throne, and was considered the legitimate ruler. The people swore allegiance to the prince and kissed the cross.

A unified consecration ritual first appeared in Russia only in the 13th–14th centuries during the Tartar-Mongol rule. The beginning of the ceremony was in the Golden Horde. The chosen prince would mount

◄— **Emperor Alexander III during the coronation in the Cathedral of the Assumption on 15 May 1883. Starting from Peter I, emperors wore the uniform of the Preobrazhensky (Transfiguration) Regiment for the coronation ceremony**

a horse and was given a charter with the Khan's seal to rule as a great prince. Proxies escorted the prince to Russia and raised him to the throne in Vladimir where the Russian metropolitans blessed their new ruler.

The princes continuously fought with each other for the right to possess a charter with the Khan's seal. In 1328, Prince of Moscow Ivan Kalita secured such a charter and became the Great Prince of Vladimir and the sole collector of levies across all of Russia. Before that Prince Ivan succeeded in persuading the Metropolitan Peter to relocate his residence from Vladimir to Moscow thus concentrating spiritual power over the Russian lands. However, following the tradition all "enthronements" of great princes continued to occur in the Cathedral of the Assumption in Vladimir, where all grand princes had to travel until Vasily II the Blind (known in Russian as Vasily the Dark) ascended the throne. After that the ceremony took place in the Cathedral of the Assumption in the Kremlin.

In 1472, Ivan III, the son of Vasily II, married a Greek princess Sophia Paleolog and adopted the Byzantine national emblem and ceremonies along with. In 1480 the rule of the Golden Horde was broken. Ivan III having become czar and ruler of all Russia put up the double eagles on the Kremlin towers, and in 1498 crowned his grandson Dmitry in accordance with the Byzantine ceremony, which he must have learned from his wife. During the ceremony an ancient "golden hat" kept in the armoury of the Moscow princes was used. It would later become the chief attribute of sovereign's powers and under the name "The Monomakh Hat" would be used as the crown for the rulers ascending the throne. It was first placed by Ivan III on the head of his grandson during the crowning ceremony. In addition, barmas — shoulder adornments that served as a symbol of power for Russian princes — were laid on Dmitry. After the liturgy the crowned Great Prince came out to Sobornaya (Cathedral) Square and was showered with gold and silver coins.

At that time, Ivan III and his spouse Sophia were quarrelling, Ivan therefore chose as his heir his son Dmitry, who was born during his first marriage. However, when the couple became reconciled with each other, and Dmitry incurred the ruler's anger, Ivan III forbade his grandson to call himself Great Prince and put him in prison where Dmitry died at the age of 25. The throne was inherited by Vasily III, Sophia's son, who chose not to be crowned in the same manner probably not wishing to temp providence.

A tale of the descent of the power of Moscow princes from Byzantine emperors started to take shape in the time of Vasily III and finalized under Ivan the Terrible, his son. In 1547, the 17-year-old Ivan arranged his own crowning ceremony for the first time in Russia, wanting to rid himself of the guardianship of the Boyars and planning large-scale reforms. At the same time the Gold Arabian Chain was added to the national regalia, and divine attributes were added to Ivan's full title in official documents.

During the ceremony held on 16 January 1547 in the Cathedral of the Assumption the word "Czar" (derived from the Latin name and title "Caesar") was first used as a title in Russia. Muscovy became a Czardom and great princes were officially named czars, which was equivalent to the western notion of an "emperor". However, this self-crowning was not quite legitimate. It is only 15 years later in 1560 that Ivan the Terrible succeeded in securing Constantinople's blessing. It was given in the form of a charter of Patriarch Joasaph II signed by 36 metropolitans

One of the scenes on the Monomakh Throne depicts Prince Vladimir Monomakh receiving the Golden Hat and other royal regalia

and bishops. In his special personal letter Patriarch of Constantinople proclaimed Ivan the Terrible "Czar and Ruler of Orthodox Christians in the entire Universe from the East to the West and to the ocean".

Ivan the Terrible formally abdicated in 1575 and enthroned Tartarian Czarevitch Simeon (Simon) from an apanage principality. "Czar" Simeon occupied the throne wearing the so-called Kazan Crown specially made for him until the spectacle bored Ivan the Terrible.

During the next crowning — of Czar Feodor, the last czar of the Rurikid Dynasty — that took place on 31 May 1584 a new royal regalia appeared — an orb or "the apple of power" made in the form of a ball topped with a cross. It symbolized power over all Orthodox lands in the world.

In the 16th century lavish festivities accompanied the crowning. Thus, festivities on the occasion of Feodor's coronation lasted the whole week and culminated with grandiose fireworks fired from 170 cannons.

During Feodor's crowning a boyar, Boris Godunov, held the orb for a long time, which turned to be symbolic as Boris eventually became czar. His crowning was especially significant because the first Russian Patriarch, Iov, performed it. Boris Godunov's heir, his unfortunate son Feodor, did not survive to ascend the throne being killed by traitors. Shah Abbas I sent a gift for his abortive crowning — a magnificent golden throne referred to as the "Persian". The False Dmitry, whose crowning was performed

The ancient Monomakh Throne in the Cathedral of the Assumption at the south wall opposite the altar

with so many mistakes that it could be hardly considered legitimate, made use of this throne. The Persian Throne was never used again on the grounds that it had been desecrated by the impostor.

The Romanovs

After the Time of Troubles and the Polish invasion, in the early 17th century only two out of seven crowns were left in the Czars' treasury — the Monomakh Hat and the Kazan Hat, which used to belong to Ivan the Terrible. Czar Mikhail, the first of the Romanov Dynasty, had to make use of some attributes of his predecessors during his crowning in 1613. Among the regalia laid on Mikhail was a breast cross with the parts of the Holy Cross of Calvary. Patriarch Philotheus sent this relic to Moscow from Constantinople in 1377.

The Diamond Hat (1682–1687) of the 11-year-old Peter I worn by him on formal occasions

Another important tradition is also associated with the crowning of the first Romanov. A new, so-called Golden Throne

Painters and sculptors often portray Ivan IV the Terrible on the Paleolog Throne made of ivory. Ivan IV and Metropolitan Philip

was made for him which was afterwards used in all the coronations of the 18th-19th centuries but was intended for empresses. Emperors used the throne that was given to Ivan III by Sophia Paleolog as her contribution to the royal regalia. In 1883, Alexander III changed the usage of these two historic relics: the Paleolog Throne was used for empresses while the Golden Throne was used for emperors. Therefore the two last Russian emperors were crowned on the throne of Czar Mikhail.

Czar Alexius who aspired to turn Moscow into the Third Rome ordered royal regalia from the Czar's City, which was what Constantinople was called in Russia although the city had born the name of Istanbul for two hundred years. In 1657–1665 by the Czar's order a new set of regalia was made of gold and emeralds. They cost 18325 rubles though the best Russian jeweler generally earned 40 rubles a year.

In 1676, Czar Alexius commissioned Nicholas Spapharius, the Russian envoy in Peking, to purchase precious stones rare in size and beauty, which was done. Some of these precious stones, including a giant spinel, later adorned the Russian crowns.

In 1682, the Monomakh Hat was used during the crowning held in the Cathedral of the Assumption for last time. It was necessary to make a replica of it because two czars — Ivan and Peter — were jointly crowned. Ivan who was older was wearing the old Hat while Peter was wearing the new, more modest one. A double silver throne and another scepter were also made for the same purpose. Both czarevitches sat on this throne under the double eagle both holding scepters to the great surprise of foreigners.

The 18th Century

Peter I having become the sole ruler changed all symbols of supreme power adapting them to the European fashion. In 1721, Russia was proclaimed an empire, and the crowning ritual was called a coronation. The golden hat adorned with fur was

Empress Anna's Crown — now features a large tourmaline instead of the Chinese spinel. Manufactured by Gotlib William Dunkel, St. Petersburg, 1731

replaced by a diamond crown, barmas were replaced by an ermine mantle or the purple, and the Golden Arabian Chain was replaced by a diamond chain of the first Russian order of the Holy Apostle Andrew.

The Monomakh Hat was carried ahead of the ceremonial procession. The former symbols of power were placed into the Armory, and the tales associated with them sank into oblivion. While previously anyone who came first and secured a place could attend the crowning ceremony in the Cathedral of the Assumption, now it was necessary to procure a ticket to get into the Kremlin, and tribunes and seats for spectators were built around the churches. Newly coronated monarchs were not showed three times with gold and silver coins any more.

Czarevitch Alexius, in accordance with

Ivan VI was a maternal great-grandson of Czar Ivan V. He was raised to the throne at the age of two months and considered Emperor in the rule of his mother Anna until 25 November 1741. He along with Peter III remained uncrowned emperors

Peter I laid the crown on Catherine's head himself but he did not hand her the scepter remaining the sole ruler. The next who was coronated with the same crown in the same manner on 25 February 1728 was his fifteen-year-old grandson Peter II.

During the era of empresses more attention was paid to the form than the meaning of the ritual. The regalia became just magnificent. In 1731, a new crown was made for Empress Anna adorned with the precious stones taken from the previous crown. Therefore the first Russian crown worn by Catherine I and Peter II which is now displayed at the Armory looks more modest than it was designed originally. Anna's crown is adorned with 2536 diamonds, 4 sapphires, 17 rubies, and 5 spinels. A huge tourmaline serves as the base for the diamond cross, and originally the crown featured a giant Chinese spinel which was taken off in 1762 to adorn the Catherine II's crown. Anna's new crown was different in shape: copying Byzantine crowns it was made of two

Empress Catherine II (coronated on 22 September 1762)

hemispheres, which symbolized the Eastern and Western Empires. All Russian crowns have followed this pattern since.

As for this one, it passed ove the uncrowned infant emperor Ivan VI to

Empress Elizabeth (coronated on 25 April 1742) introduced new regalia into practice — the state banner, the state sword, and the ceremonial seal

the law on succession to the throne, could have been the first Russian emperor coronated with the new regalia. However, in 1718, at the insistence of Peter I he disavowed his rights to the throne before the Icon of Our Lady of Vladimir in the Cathedral of the Assumption. Therefore, the first one who was coronated in a new fashion was Catherine I for whom the Russian European-type crown was made of gilded silver adorned with diamonds and gems (all in all, 2500 stones).

Elizabeth, Peter I's daughter. Traditionally, gracious decrees were dated for the coronation. This time capital punishment was banned in Russia. New regalia appeared in the ritual — the state banner, the state sword, and the so-called ceremonial seal. After Elizabeth nobody used her crown. In 1762, Catherine II commissioned a new crown for herself that was intended to outshine all the previous ones. The court jeweler Jeremiah Posier made it by selecting the best stones from all the adornments available in the emperors' treasury to create a "diamond symphony" out of them within two months. To adorn the crown he used 58 large and 4878 small diamonds, a giant precious spinel taken off Anna's crown, and over fifty large pearls. No European monarch had such a crown, and since then the Great Crown of the Russian Empire was used in all coronations.

In the reign of Paul I the coronation ceremony was modified. In 1797, for the first time along with the emperor his spouse Maria was coronated, which corresponded to the ancient Byzantine tradition. The Small Imperial Crown modeled after the Great Crown was made for her. Besides the Small Crown, which was used for coronation only, the imperial couple acquired the right to wear the so-called outing crowns on formal occasions. Afterwards they were destroyed, and the gems were given away in accordance with the will.

Later, in 1801, another Small Crown

The famous Orlov Diamond on the Imperial Scepter is one of the largest diamonds in the world (189.6 carats)

The Maltese Crown of Emperor Paul I. Paul I received this crown along with the title of the Great Master of the Order of John of Jerusalem in 1798

was made for the spouse of Alexander I Elizabeth, and it is this crown that all subsequent rulers coronated their spouses with. It was the crown that Nicholas II laid on his wife Alexandra.

The Orlov Diamond on a Gold Scepter and the Gold Orb

Catherine II enriched the Russian regalia with one more relic — a gold scepter with the Orlov diamond, one of the largest in the world. The Emperor Paul I was the first who was coronated with this scepter. Afterwards it was used in the coronations of all emperors.

The diamond was a gift given to Catherine II by Count Grigory Orlov. According to the legend, it was one of two famous stones that served as eyes for an Indian idol in the Vishnu Temple near Madras. After travelling a lot all over the world it ended up in the hands of a famous wealthy Armenian Lazarev who traded in diamonds. Count Orlov purchased the diamond from him for 400,000 rubles. This amount was more than twice as large as the official annual income of the Count but his plan was worth more than just money. The largest diamond in the world at that time was given to Catherine on her name day. Soon it was displayed on the state scepter, and Orlov's name was immortalized in the name of this diamond.

Emperor Paul I was coronated in the Cathedral of the Assumption on 4 April 1797. Instead of the Maltese cross he wore the symbol of the Order of St. Andrew

For the coronation of Catherine II a new royal orb was also made. It represented a polished gold ball on a small pedestal. It took its final shape in the reign of Paul I.

A new tradition was set during the coronation of Paul I: copying Peter the Great he ascended the throne dressed in the uniform of the Preobrazhensky (Transfiguration) Regiment, which became mandatory for all subsequent emperors. Later a unique Maltese Crown would be added to Emperor Paul's regalia which he would receive in 1798 along with other relics of the order of St. John of Jerusalem from the Knights Hospitallers who selected him to be their Great Master.

The 19th century

The coronation of Alexander I in 1801 reflected the young emperor's enthusiasm in mysticism.

On 9 September at 9 o'clock in the morning nine cannon shots and ringing of the bells of Ivan the Great Bell Tower announced that the imperial procession was approaching the city gate. The coronation itself took place on 15 September. It was at that time but 11 years later that Napoleon occupied the Kremlin, and in the middle of

Portrait of the Emperor Alexander I (1825) painted by George Dawe

the Cathedral of the Assumption instead of the coronation platform a furnace was put to melt the church silverware.

Nicholas I was the only Russian monarch who was twice coronated: in 1826 in Moscow and in 1829 in Warsaw as Czar of Poland. The period between ascending the throne and coronation was unusually long — eight months. It took that long to suppress the armed uprising of a group of revolutionary-minded nobles, punish the instigators and wait until the political unrest had calmed down.

Portrait of the Grand Prince and future Emperor Nikolas I (1820s) painted by George Dawe

Alexander II was coronated in 1856. According to a reporter of the London Times, his coronation was a blend of the profusion of the Roman Caesars and the elegance of the West. At the same time, as the reporter noted, Russia took the occasion to demonstrate in an unusual way its military might. The parade of warriors in splendid national attire was "like a dream from A Thousand and One Nights. The Imperial escort of Caucasians on thoroughbred fleet-footed steeds wearing chain amours of the 18th century, Bashkirs with lances on shaggy horses, stately Black-Sea Cossacks in sheepskin hats, Abkhazians in amours and fine chain amours, wild mountaineers and residents of such places where a European educated man had never been. The Emperor who was named "Liberator" for abolishing serfdom was killed by a terrorist in 1881.

The coronation of Alexander III that took place two years later was held with increased security precautions but it did not spoil the celebration. Traditional illumination of the Kremlin was supplemented with a technical innovation: Ivan the Great Bell Tower was illuminated with innumerable electric lights, and the whole ancient ensemble looked like a fairy-tale marvel. The public was treated to unprecedented in

Portrait of the Emperor Alexander III (1880s)

lavishness food, drinks and gifts. Shortly after the coronation on 26 May 1883 the monarch and his family attended the consecration of the Church of Christ the Savior which was blown up during the Soviet rule, in 1931, and rebuilt in 2000.

Almost four hundred years after the

first crowning ceremony held in the Kremlin, in 1896, the coronation of Emperor Nicholas II took place there in the Cathedral of the Assumption. It was the most splendid in the entire history of Russia and the last one.

The State Regalia

Since 18th century, when St. Petersburg became the capital city, the main state regalia (including both Imperial Crowns, the orb, the scepter and two order chains of the order of Holy Apostle Andrew) were kept there and brought to Moscow only for coronations. The two ancient thrones were permanently kept in the Kremlin, at the Armory. The purples were usually made for each coronation.

For formal ceremonies and receptions the monarchs used other regalia. These regalia were also worshipped. In the 17th century, they were stored in oak chests under the royal seal, which was believed to protect them from "the evil eye." However, they were not as important historically as the coronation regalia. As of 2 March 1917 (the date when Nicholas II abdicated), the state regalia included:

1. The Great Imperial Crown
2. The Small Imperial Crown
3. The Scepter with the Double Eagle
4. The Orb
5. The Purples or Imperial Mantles (2 items)
6. The Great and the Small Chains of the Order of Holy Apostle Andrew and two stars of the order (4 items)
7. The State Banner
8. The State Shield with the Sword
9. The State Ceremonial Seal
10. The Emperor Throne
11. The Empress Throne

At present the regalia of the last Emperor and Empress as well as of other Russian monarchs (except the seal whose whereabouts is unknown) are exhibited at the Armory (in windows in Rooms #6 and #7) and at the Diamond Depository.

Symbols of royal power in the 16th–17th centuries

**Czar Boris Godunov
(ruled in 1598–1605)**

1. **Royal crown**
2. **Shoulder barmas**
3. **Pectoral cross with the fragments of the Holy Cross of Calvary**
4. **Scepter**
5. **Orb**

Another symbol of power — the gold Monomakh chain is not depicted on the portrait

Symbols of royal power in the 18th–20th centuries

**Emperor Nicholas II
(ruled in 1894–1917)**

1. **Great Imperial Crown**
2. **Imperial Mantle**
3. **Diamond chain of the Order of the St. Apostle Andrew**
4. **Star of the Order of the St. Apostle Andrew**
5. **Scepter with one of largest diamonds in the world — the Orlov Diamond**
6. **Orb**

Symbols of Power

According to one of the official historic
legends dating back to the 16th century, it
is believed that the symbols of power which
were used in crowning ceremonies before
Peter the Great were brought to Russia from
Byzantium. These symbols include:

1. The Monomakh Hat
2. Emperor August's Bowl
3. Gold barmas (medallions with images
of saints attached to shoulders)
4. The Orb
5. The Gold Chain.

According to this version, the regalia
(or at least some of them) were passed
to grand prince Vladimir Monomakh
(1052–1125) by his maternal grandfather
Constantine IX Monomachos. Although
Constantine IX had died fifty years before
Vladimir became Prince of Kiev, the gift
on his behalf could have been sent from
Constantinople much later.

**Prince of Kiev
Vladimir Mono-
makh (1052–
1125), born
to Vsevolod I
and Byzantine
Czarevna Maria,
daughter of Czar
Constantine IX
Monomachos**

The Monomakh Hat

The Monomakh Hat is made of eight gold
plates. Each is decorated with open-work
gold wire, precious stones and pearls. The
Hat is topped with a cross whose ends are
adorned with pearls. At the base of the cross
are stones: a ruby, blue and yellow sapphires
and large pearls.

Historians reckon that the Hat was
made in the Orient in the 13th–14th centuries. The upper part with the gold cross must
have been added to the older basement in
the 15th–16th centuries in the time of Ivan III
or Ivan the Terrible. In the Middle Ages it
was common to make oriental artifacts look
Christian. The original mother-of-pearls and
gold pendants were replaced by the adorn-
ment of sable fur, which was more typical
for Russia. The fur had to be replaced several
times. The Hat weighs 698 grams.

**The Monomakh Hat — the
first royal crown. The Russian
czars from Ivan the Terrible to
Peter I were crowned with this
Hat as part of their coronation**

It is
believed that
Prince of
Moscow Ivan
Kalita actu-
ally received
the Mono-
makh Hat as
a gift along
with the
charter for
Grand Prin-
cipality in
1327 or 1328
from Khan
Uzbek. It was

worn only once — during the crowning. On
other occasions each monarch used to have
his own crown.

The Great and the Small Imperial Crowns

Both crowns are stored at the Diamond Depository. The Great Crown is made of gilded
silver. A crude dark-red precious stone (called
"spinel") installed
at the top is the
most valuable of
the stones pur-
chased for Czar
Alexius in China
in the 17th cen-
tury. It consists
of 398.72 carats.
The diamond
scattered on the
entire surface of
the crown form
symbolic images
of palm and lau-
rel leaves, and on
the arch between
two hemispheres

**Great Imperial Crown
(1762). Was used for the
coronation of russian monarchs from Catherine II to
Nikolas II**

are oak leaves with acorns. At the front, the
arch is adorned with three almond-shaped
diamonds and one diamond octagonal at
the base. The lower garland surrounding
the crown features 27 large diamonds and
numerous small ones. At the edges of the
arch both hemispheres are bordered with
two rows of dim pearls, 27 in each row. The
crown is lined with a purple velvet hat. The
height to the top of the cross is about 19.5
cm, the height of the stone with the cross is
about 6.5 cm, and the diameter of the crown
ranges from 14.5 to 15.5 cm. Its weight is
about 2 kg.

The Small Crown was modeled on
the Great Imperial Crown and is similarly
made of silver. It is adorned with large and

Small Imperial Crown (1801). Was used for the coronation of emperors' wives in the 19th century. (Another small crown was used in coronation of Paul I's wife)

small diamonds, including 22 select diamonds placed on the surrounding garland. The crown is topped with a diamond cross on a base in the shape of a diamond ring. Unlike the Great Crown the Small Crown is not adorned with other precious stones and pearls, and there are no laurel or other leaves in its diamond pattern. The crown therefore does not represent the symbol of independent power and shows that its bearer is subordinate to the Emperor. The crown was made in 1801. It is quite small in size, its height with the cross is about 10.5 cm, and it is about 12 cm in diameter.

The Symbols of the Imperial Crown

The precious spinel in the Great Imperial Crown (1762) symbolizes a grain of pomegranate, which was considered a holy fruit and the emblem of the Sun. These dark-red stones that are sometimes mistakenly called rubies also adorned earlier Russian regalia, including the Monomakh Hat.

From time immemorial, pearls with gold have been used to adorn artifacts used in religious rituals. They were associated with white, symbolizing wisdom and purity of thoughts. The palm branches made of diamonds also have a Christian meaning although Christians took the palm branch as a symbol of victory and peace from Ancient Greece. Upon his coming to Jerusalem the Savoir was greeted by the locals

Princely barmas from the Ryazan treasure, the 12th century. Were found in 1822 in the mount in the vicinity of Old Ryazan

with palm branches as lord and master on Earth.

Diamonds also form laurel wreaths and oak leaves. As it is known, in Ancient Greece and Rome the laurel symbolized glory. Since the ancient world had been considered the emblem of power and courage. However, both Eastern and Western Churches alike did not acknowledge these symbols and did not depict them on holy objects for a long time. However, in the 19th century oak and laurel were rehabilitated and came into use again. They were used for the first time in 1804 by Napoleon I in his crown. He was followed by other monarchs who began gradually to renovate their regalia. Russia followed suit in the reign of Alexander II. In 1865, the crown was dismantled and after weighing all its diamonds, a new floral pattern was made from them. On 24 July 1882 an oak branch was added to the Great State Coat of Arms of the Russian Empire on the left-hand side to complement the laurel branch on the right-hand side.

The Orb

The Orb of the Russian Empire consists of a gold ball surrounded by a rim with a semi-circle topped with a cross. The rim is made of a blue sapphire scattered with diamonds to form laurel leaves. The Orb is topped with a diamond cross with a Ceylon sapphire (200 carats), and at the crossing of the rim and the arch there is a diamond (46.92 carats). Its height is 23 cm.

The orb is the second most significant symbol of royal power (it had been used since the time of the Roman Caesars). It can be assumed that it was shaped after the pomegranate, which was an ancient symbol of life in the Orient and in the ancient world. In heraldry

Czar Mikhail Romanov's Orb, 1628. Russian emperors and empresses held this orb during their crowning in the 17th — early 18th centuries. The scenes from the life of the biblical king, King David, are depicted on the four sides of the orb

Ascending the Throne

the pomegranate was traditionally made of gold, hence the golden color of the orb. The orb in the left hand meant that Emperor supports the peaceful rule of Christianity.

The Scepter

The Scepter featuring the famous Orlov Diamond is made of pure gold and surrounded by two diamond rims. The diamond is topped with a double eagle coated with black enamel. On the chest of the eagle a horseman striking a dragon is depicted — a historic emblem of Ivan III, Prince of Moscow (sometimes this horseman is mistakenly taken for St. George). The image of the horseman is surrounded by the chain of the St. Andrew Order worn during the coronation. The height of the Scepter is 60 cm.

A scepter is also an ancient symbol of supreme power and the third in significance after the royal crown and the orb. During the coronation the Russian Emperor took the Scepter with his right hand, which meant that he was going to rule the country as a Christian and protect it from the enemies.

Mikhail Romanov's Scepter, the 17th century

Imperial Mantles or the Purples

The Imperial Mantles for the Emperor and the Empress were made of golden silk (brocart glacé), adorned with images of double eagles embroidered by hand, and lined with ermine fur.

Peter I replicated the coronation mantles or the purples for himself and his spouse following a western European design. In western royal dynasties ermine symbolized innocence and chastity. According to a legend, this animal chose to die rather than let its snow-white fur become blemished.

On the other hand, the purple with its wide ermine collar evidently is reminiscent of the ancient Russian garment worn for the enthronement ceremony.

The Symbol of the Order of St. Apostle Andrew on the Chain and the Order Star

The large chain of the Order of St. Andrew displayed at the Diamond Depository was made in the reign of Catherine II in about 1795. It consists of 20 three-type images: a double eagle under the crown, the Cross

St. Apostle Andrew is considered a holy patron of Russia. Some of his relics used to be kept in the Cathedral of the Assumption

of St. Andrew with Latin letters SAPR (Latin acronym meaning St. Andrew Patron of Russia) and Peter I's monogram set in a frame of military banners. The chain holds the symbol of the Order — a double eagle with spread wings and topped with a crown, and a blue enamel cross with crucified Apostle Andrew and the same letters SAPR. All parts and sections are scattered with diamonds of different sizes that is why the chain is sometimes called the Diamond. It is 1.5 m long. During a coronation the emblem on the chain was worn on top of the Imperial purple.

The look of symbols of royal power in Russia changed over the centuries. The cross with some relics (the 16th–17th centuries) and the symbol of the Order of St. Andrew with a fragment of the chain (the late 18th century).

In the middle of the diamond star of the Order there is a double eagle. It is surrounded by the motto of the Order: "For Trust and Loyalty".

A legend says that the St. Apostle Andrew back in the 1st century A.D. placed a cross in the vicinity of modern Kiev thus predetermining the christening of Russia which happened on the banks of the Dnieper almost a thousand years later. Since then the

The banner of the time of Czar Alexius I (17th century)

The State Banner of Russia (early 20th century)

Apostle has been considered to be one of the patrons of Russia. (Besides Russia St. Andrew is considered to be patron of Greece and Scotland.) Therefore Peter I set up the first Russian order in 1698 in his honor. On the Order St. Andrew is depicted crucified in the shape of the letter X. He requested to that he be crucified in such a manner that his death should not be reminiscent of the sufferings of Jesus.

The State Banner

The banners consists of a breadth of cloth on a staff with two memorial ribbons. On both sides of the golden fabric there was a

The Russian banner of the time of the Kazan campaign of Ivan the Terrible (16th century)

double eagle with title emblems surrounded by other emblems connected by palm and oak branches. The staff bore a double eagle and ribbons with captions «862, 988», «1497, 1721». The first two dates signified the year of foundation of Russia when legendary Prince Rurikid was called and the year when St. Prince Vladimir christened Russia. The other two dates signified the year when the first code of laws was published in Russia (Sudebnik of Ivan III) and the year when Russia was proclaimed empire. The staff is 3.3 m tall. The size of the banner cloth is 155 cm x 165 cm.

The banner was added to the state regalia under Elizabeth, the daughter of Peter the Great, in the 1740s. In the time of Ivan the Terrible there was a military banner depicting the image of Christ, and in the reign of Czar Alexius there was a banner depicting the Czar himself on horseback in military uniform.

The State Shield and Sword

The State Sword, sheath and shield were manufactured during the reign of Czar Alexius in the late 17th century as a symbol of indivisible unity of the Romanov Dynasty with the Russian Throne. The Sword is 98 cm long, including the hilt, which is 38 cm long. Closer to the hilt on one side of the blade, a gold double eagle holding a writhing dragon in his claws is embossed, on the other side — a griffin with an unsheathed sword, the symbol of the Romanov Dynasty. The end of the sword hilt is made of two eagle heads under the Monomakh Hat, and the crosspiece features two griffin heads on a long neck looking upwards and downwards. The sheath is upholstered with gold silk

The State Sword with Sheath and the Shield

The ancient Gold throne of Czar Mikhail was used for coronation of emperors and empresses of the Romanovs Dynasty in the 18th–19th centuries

Royal Thrones

All three main Russian thrones used in coronations look very similar though they were manufactured by different masters in different periods. In the 18th–19th centuries the Gold Throne of Czar Mikhail Romanov was used for the coronation of empresses and emperors. It is a hard chair made in the traditional Russian style with a high back and arm rests. However, the throne is rich in ornamentation. It is coated with gold plates whose total weight comes to about 13 kg and decorated with 1964 precious stones. The throne is 154 cm tall, 75 cm wide, and 52 cm long.

Probably the throne was a gift given to Ivan the Terrible. Its oriental look matched the Monomakh Hat and other vestments traditionally belonging to the Czar. It looked archaic with the European crown and the ermine purple. However, it continued to be used in coronations even in the 19th century.

The so-called Diamond Throne made in Iran in the second half of the 17th century was given to Czar Alexius by an Ar-

(brocart glacé). The round shield made of wood is upholstered with red velvet on both sides and adorned with decorations made of nephrite, rock crystal, precious stones, and stained glass in gold and silver medallions. The shield was not used in coronations but it was carried in Imperial funeral processions.

menian trade company as a "complement" to an application for the right to trade with Russia. The Czar took a liking to the throne.

The throne is made of sandalwood with gold and silver plates. It is decorated with 876 diamonds, 1223 sapphires, turquoise and pearls, hence the name of the throne. On the back there is an image of two large effeminate Oriental angels with wings of multicolored plumes who support a kind of a crown under a dedicatory inscription in Latin. Later three gold figurines were added to the back and

The Diamond Throne of the time of Czar Alexius I, 17th century

the side crossbars — a double eagle in the center, the Apostle Peter on the left and St. Nicholas on the right. On the lower crossbar of the throne there is an image of a procession of elephants symbolizing stability and wellbeing. The throne is 161 cm tall, 75.5 cm wide, and 51 cm long.

The other throne is made of wood in Western Europe (the 16th century) and faced with plates of carved ivory and walrus bone. The inventory of the czar's treasury of the 17th century does not have any records about when and where this throne was made and how it came to Russia. It is believed that it was sent to Ivan III from Rome as a marriage portion of the Greek princess Sophia who was recommended to him by a Catholic Cardinal of Greek descent Vissarion. At any rate, the throne was evidently russified in later years: a double eagle with imperial regalia on the back was added much later and does not match its European counterparts — a unicorn and a lion.

Probably the first one to use this throne was Ivan III

The first Russian throne made of ivory of the time of Ivan III sent from Rome, early 16th century

The throne given to Boris Godunov in 1604 by Shah Abbas

when crowning his grandson Dmitry in 1498. Afterwards it was used by Ivan the Terrible and other monarchs of both genders.

Another throne was a gift of Shah Abbas given to Czar Boris Godunov in 1604. Persian masters were able to turn a stool with a low back into almost a piece of jewelry art. The throne preserved its original design because the first Romanovs preferred to ignore all things associated with Boris Godunov. The throne is adorned with 2300 precious stones, mainly rubies, pearls and is colored in varied shades of turquoise.

Augustus's Bowl

This jasper bowl with a jade viper on the lid was not an official symbol, and yet was always featured in the rite. According to a legend, the bowl used to belong to the Roman Emperor Augustus. The snake on the lid had a special meaning. On Emperor Augustus's scepter, the snake was displayed underneath the eagle as a symbol of wisdom and eternity. On the other hand, the snake has symbolized good health in the Christian tradition, harking back to the Middle East. In Russia, bowls with snake images were used to keep myrrh, the Holy Oil that "heals the body and the soul."

According to the same legend, Byzantine Emperors had inherited Augustus's Bowl from Rome. Eventually it ended up in the hands

Augustus's Bowl. The look from both sides

of Vladimir Monomakh and the Princes of Muscovy. All Russian monarchs, from Ivan the Terrible to Nicholas II, were anointed with myrrh from this bowl at coronation. The current whereabouts of the bowl are unknown.

The coronation of Nicholas I on 22 August 1826. During the prayer on behalf of the nation all except the sovereign, who bore the orb and the scepter, kneeled down

Russian Czars, Emperors and Empresses crowned at the Cathedral of the Assumption

(dates according to the old calendar; rulers marked with an "*" were never crowned).

Dmitry (1483–1509), the son of Prince Ivan, Greatson of Great Prince Ivan III, was the first Russian ruler to be officially crowned on 4 February 1498 at age 15. However, his title was all he ever inherited from his Greatfather.

Ivan IV, "Ivan the Terrible" (1530–1584), the son of Vasily III and Elena Glinskaya, was

the first Russian ruler to self-apply the title of "Czar of Moscow and All Russia." Ivan IV, who was Great Prince under Boyar rule from 1533 to 1547, was crowned on 16 January 1547 at age 17, and reigned until 18 March 1584.

Feodor (1557–1598), the son of Ivan IV and Anastasia Zakharyina-Yurieva, was crowned on 31 May 1584 at age 27, and reigned from 19 March 1584 to 7 January 1598. He was the last descendant of the House of Rurik, which had ruled Russia since the 9th century.

Boris Godunov (1552–1605), the son of Feodor Ivanovich, a boyar from the ancient

Godunov family, was the first Russian Czar elected by the popular Land Assembly in February 1598. Crowned on 1 September 1598 at age 46. Reigned from 21 February 1598 to 13 April 1605.

Feodor II Godunov* (1589–1605), the son of Boris Godunov and Maria Skuratova-Belskaya. Reigned from 14 April 1605 to 10 June 1605. Feodor II reigned for only two months and was never crowned before he was assassinated by a Boyar conspiracy.

Dmitry the Impostor, aka. Grigory Otrepiev (?– 1606), impersonated Czarevich Dmitry, the son of Ivan the Terrible and Maria Nagaya, who had died in Uglich in 1591 under mysterious circumstances. The impostor was accepted by Muscovites and crowned on 30 July 1605, but did not last very long on the throne. He was deposed and assassinated on 17 May 1606.

Vasily IV (Vasily Shuisky) (1547–1610), the son of Prince Ivan Shuisky, elected on 19 May 1606, crowned on 1 June 1606 at age 59. Reigned until 12 September 1612, when he was deposed by Boyars and forced into monasticism. Hermogenus, who was then Patriarch, never accepted Vasily's monastic vows. Vasily IV was eventually buried as a secular Czar at the Cathedral of the Archangels.

Mikhail I (1596–1645), the son of Boyar Feodor Romanov-Yuriev and nephew

of Czarina Anastasia and Xenia Shestova, was the first Romanov on the Russian throne, elected by the Land Assembly on 21 February 1613, and crowned on 11 July 1613 at age 16. Reigned until 12 July 1645.

Alexius I (1629–1676), the son of Mikhail Feodorovich and Eudochia Streshneva, was crowned on 28 September 1645 at age 16, and reigned from 13 July 1645 to 29 January 1676.

Feodor III (1656–1682), the son of Alexius Mikhailovich and Maria Miloslavskaya, was crowned on 18 June 1676 at age 20, and reigned from 30 January 1676 to 27 April 1682.

Ivan V (1666–1689), another son of

Alexius Mikhailovich and Maria Miloslavskaya, was Czar in name only from 26 May 1682 to 29 January 1696, when Czarina Sophia was the de facto ruler. Crowned together with his brother Peter on 25 June 1682 at age 16.

Peter I, "the Great" (1672–1725), the son of Alexius Mikhailovich and Natalia Naryshkina, was proclaimed Czar on 27 April 1682. After his brother Ivan died, Peter reigned solely from 29 January 1696 to 28 January

1725. Crowned together with his brother Ivan on 25 June 1682 at age 10. Peter I was the first Russian ruler to accept the title of Russian Emperor on 21 October 1721 at the Trinity Cathedral in St. Petersburg. From then

on, Russia became an empire, and Russian Czars – emperors. However, Peter himself was never re-crowned as Emperor after his only coronation as Czar on 25 June 1682.

Catherine I (1684–1727), nee Martha Skvaronskaya, of common descent. Peter the Great's second wife. Crowned on 7 May 1724 at age 40. Reigned from 28 January 1725 (when Peter the Great died) to 6 May 1727.

Peter II (1715–1730), the son of Czarevich Alexius Petrovich and Crown Princess

Charlotte of Braunschweig and Wolfenbuttel, was crowned on 25 February 1728 at age 12, and reigned from 7 May 1727 to 19 January 1730. Peter II was the last direct male descendant of the House of Romanov.

Anna Johannovna (1693–1740), the daughter of Ivan V and Praskovia Saltykova, was crowned on 28 April 1730 at age 37, and reigned from 19 January 1730 to 17 October 1740.

Ivan VI* (1740–1764), the son of Anton-Ulrich, the Prince of Braunschweig, and Anna Leopoldovna, the Princess of Mecklenburg, and Anna Johannovna's nephew, was proclaimed Emperor on 17 October 1740 at age two months, while his mother was the de facto ruler until 25 November 1741. Ivan VI was never crowned and died in prison.

Elizabeth (1709–1761), the daughter of Peter I and Catherine I, was crowned on 25 April 1742 at age 32, and reigned from 26 November 1741 to 25 December 1761.

Peter III* (1728–1762), aka. Karl-Peter-Ulrich, the son of Karl Friedrich, the Duke of Schleswig-Holstein, and Peter I's daughter

Czarina Anna, converted to Orthodox Christianity at the Church of the Assumption. Did not reign long enough to be crowned before being ousted by his wife Catherine. Reigned from 26 December 1761 to 28 June 1762.

Catherine II, "the Great" (1729–1796), nee Sophia-Augusta-Frederica, the Princess of Anhalt-Zerbst, married Peter III in 1745, was crowned on 22 September 1762 at age 33, and reigned from 28 June 1762 to 6 November 1796.

Paul I (1754–1801), the son of Peter III and Catherine II, was crowned on 4 April 1797 at age 42, and reigned from 6 November 1796 to 11 March 1801.

Alexander I "the Blessed" (1777–1825), the son of Paul I and Maria Feodorovna, was crowned on 15 September 1801 at age 23, and reigned from 12 March 1801 to 19 November 1825.

Nicholas I "the Unforgettable" (1796–1855), the son of Paul I and Maria Feodorovna, was the only Russian monarch

to be crowned twice, first in Moscow on 22 August 1826 as the Emperor of Russia at age 30, then in Warsaw on 12 May 1829 as the King of Poland. Reigned from 14 December 1825 to 18 February 1855.

Alexander II "the Liberator" (1818–1881), the son of Nicholas I and Alexandra Feodorovna, was crowned on 26 August 1856 at age 38, and reigned from 19 February 1855 to 1 March 1881.

Alexander III "the Peacemaker" (1845–1894), the son of Alexander II and Maria Alexandrovna, was coronated on 15 May 1883 at age 38, and reigned from 2 March 1881 to 20 October 1894.

St. Nicholas II "the Martyr" (1868–1918), the son of Alexander III and Maria Feodorovna, was coronated on 14 May 1896 at age 28, and reigned from 20 October 1894 to 2 March 1917.

Ascending the Throne

Arkhangelsky sobor
(Cathedral of the Archangel Michael)

Standing tall on the crest of Borovitsky Hill in the southeastern part of Cathedral Square, the Cathedral of the Archangel Michael is clearly visible from many points, but the best view is from the Moskva River. The Cathedral is the largest royal necropolis in Russia, housing the graves of all Princes and Czars who died between 1340 and 1696, the only later exception being Emperor Peter II, who died in 1730.

There is evidence that, in the mid-13th century, there was a wooden church on this spot, dedicated to Archangel Michael who, according to Christian beliefs, guards the Gates of Paradise. In 1333, Prince Ivan Kalita ordered a new stone church built here to serve as a burial vault for the princes. Kalita himself became the

Archangel Michael, leader of the celestial army and guardian of the Gates of Paradise. House icon of the Cathedral of the Archangel Michael, late 14th century

first ruler of Muscovy to be buried in the new Cathedral. Prince Daniil, who had died 30 years before Kalita, was buried at the St. Daniel Monastery, which he had founded not far from the Kremlin.

There are 53 graves under the floorboards of the Cathedral, with 46 tombstones above them. The murals portray the rulers buried here, along with earlier Russian rulers from the 9th to 16th centuries.

Russian princes and Czars used to come to the Cathedral on memorial days — Trinity (Parents') Saturday, Easter, Radonitsa and others. They also came here when they were about to go to war or embark on a pilgrimage to some far-off monastery, and during coronation. The rulers made lavish "soul pence" donations to the church — holy vessels, jewel-set Gospels and icon decorations.

← **The reading of acathistus for the Holy Czarevich Dmitry at the shrine containing his relics**

The graves of Ivan the Terrible and his two sons always attract the most visitor attention. It is believed that Czarevich Ivan was killed by his father in a fit of rage after a bitter altercation. The other Czarevich — Feodor — ended the Rurik line of rulers (with the exception of Vasily Shuisky), who had run Russia for seven and a half centuries. These graves are behind the altar barrier, next to the southerly wall: one cannot get close to them.

After the Voznesensky (Ascension) Church was pulled down in 1929, 35 tombs of Russian Czarinas and princesses were transferred to the Cathedral of the Archangel Michael, but are not accessible for the public.

Similarly to the Cathedral of the Assumption (Uspensky), the five domes of the Cathedral of the Archangel Michael symbolize Christ and the four Evangelists. There is only one active altar, dedicated to the Archangel Michael and other Disembodied Celestial Forces. But the Cathedral has previously housed other altars, dedicated to the Nativity of St. John the Precursor, St. Uarus, the Intercession of Our Lady, the Resurrection, Apostle Aquila, Simeon the Pillarist, and St. Andrew of Crete. The sons of Prince Ivan Kalita were namesakes of St. Simeon the Pillarist and St. Andrew of Crete. On St. Aquila Memorial Day, four thousand Moscow troops defeated 40,000 Novgorodians in the battle of the Shelon River in 1471, when Russia was torn apart by internal rivalry. The Resurrection altar, arranged as promised by the Moscow military leaders before the battle, was also consecrated in honor of that victory. The Cathedral currently hosts divine services on its saints' days — Archangel Michael Day (21 November), Memory Days of the Chernigov Miracle-Workers (27 February and 3 October), St. Czarevich Dmitry Days (28 May and 16 June), and Holy Prince Dmitry Donskoi Day (1 June).

Arkhangelsky sobor

Cathedral Decorations

On the outside, the Cathedral has changed very little over the five centuries. In fact, it looks closer to the original now than it did in the 19th century, after they removed the faux gothic porch from the church's northerly façade and demolished the fence with guardhouses around the Cathedral Square in the 1920s. The easterly façade looks quite strange: the huge stone buttresses cover a half of the southerly wall. The buttresses were installed to prop up the walls in the 1770s, when Catherine the Great was empress. During site preparation for an enormous palace nearby, the Cathedral nearly slid off the hill. There are two tiny Chapels at either end of the altar wall, added during the reign of Ivan the Terrible in the late 16th century.

The Cathedral's architect, Aloisius the New, was both an architect and a sculptor in his native Italy, but his architectural career gained preeminence at the court of Khan Mengli-Girei in the Crimea, where he designed and decorated a part of the Bakhchisarai Palace. In Moscow, they gave Aloisius the nickname "New" to distinguish him from Aloisius Friazin, the other Italian architect who had built the Kremlin walls and royal chambers. Aloisius the New began working on the Cathedral in 1505. Aloisius didn't want to take any chances with spatial design, so he just copied the layout of the Cathedral of the Assumption, and devoted most of his creative zeal to decoration. The result was a rather peculiar structure that sparked some controversy among the contemporaries. First off, the church looks more like a regular Renaissance-era Italian palazzo than a temple, the only difference being the domes. The architect dicorated the façades with seashells of white stone. His argument was that a seashell is a symbol of Virgin Mary, giving birth to Christ like a seashell gives birth to a pearl. The poetic metaphor was appreciated. In later years, Russian architects would borrow seashells and other decorative features from the Cathedral of the Archangel Michael.

Before you go in, take a good look at the Chapels — a reminder of some tragic events. In 1581, Ivan the Terrible buried his son Ivan in the southeasterly Chapel, which was then

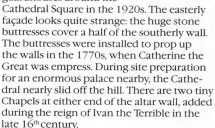

The architect placed one of his signature decorative seashells even at the High Place above the altar

consecrated in the name of St. John of the Ladder, the Czarevich's celestial patron, and memorial services for the Czarevich would be held here. Ivan the Terrible had the northwesterly Chapel built in the name of the Intercession of Our Lady, after his troops took the city of Kazan the next day after Protection Day. In the mid-19th century, the icon of the Holy Martyr Uarus and holy vessels from his altar in the dismantled Church of John the Precursor by Borovitsky Gate, were transferred to the Intercession Chapel. The Intercession Chapel was re-consecrated in the name of St. Uarus. It was customary to pray to this saint about the health of small children, and about all infants who died before they could be baptized. The custom changed in the 20th century, when St. Uarus became the saint for all those who were never baptized. His icon remained here until 1917. It's current location is not known.

There is another — unseemly but historic — annex at the southerly wall. It's the former Judgment Annex. Many centuries ago, when the Cathedral of the Archangel Michael owned land and 18,000 peasant serfs, this is where debtors were punished, who were behind on their tribute payments. They were held in the cellars, and interrogated in

Westerly entrance to the Cathedral

Murals of the Cathedral. The view of the westerly wall

Gospel scenes dominate the paintings in the vaults.

The murals on the westerly wall depict the Symbol of Faith, the fundamentals of Orthodox Christian teachings: the Lord, Jesus Christ, the Creation, the Nativity, the Crucifixion, the Ascension, scenes of the Judgment Day, and so on. The southerly and northerly walls depict the miracles of Archangel Michael. The miracle of Eunuch the Righteous being taken to Heaven in his physical body is displayed above the top window on the southerly wall, next to the iconostasis. On either side of the same window, Archangel Michael is shown holding the hand of Abraham, who is about to sacrifice his son to the Lord, and Archangel Michael fighting Jacob. The scene closer to the westerly wall is of the Archangel scorching the sinful towns of Sodom and Gomorrah with fire, after removing the promise keepers Lot and his daughters to safety. In another scene, the Archangel assists in the taking of the city of Jericho, the walls of which collapsed from the sound of the Archangel's trumpet. There is also a scene glorifying the victory of Israeli general Gedeon and his 300 unarmed soldiers over more numerous, overpowering enemy troops. Archangel Michael was believed to have appeared to Prophet Daniel in the Lion Moat, and to three adolescents — in a burning furnace. One of the murals on the southerly wall illustrates the story of a boy who found some gold and told the monastery prior about it. The prior sent three monks with the boy to collect the treasure, but the monks succumbed to the tempta-

the Judgment Annex. Before the Napoleon invasion, there was an oak table with chains and other "instruments of punishment" in the annex. The stairs lead from the annex to the cellar, which now houses the tombs of Russian Czarinas and princesses.

There are two side doors in the westerly façade alongside the main entrance, leading down to the church vestry in the basement, and to the inner Chapels. In the 16th–17th centuries the Czarinas and princesses stayed in these Chapels during sermons.

The Cathedral looks dark and cramped inside. Little light seeps in through the narrow windows high above. Four massive pillars support the vaults. Most of the space is occupied by tombstones.

Unlike its façades, the church's interior appears to be fairly traditional for old Russian churches. The interior forms a single space with all the walls, vaults and pillars covered with murals. The first murals were ordered by Ivan the Terrible. In 1652, when Alexius was Czar, the shabby 16th century frescoes were copied and removed, but further work was suspended. The new murals were painted in 1666, mostly repeating the original frescoes. The new murals have since undergone a succession of renovations.

The frescoes show the princes with halos above their heads. Inside the spheres next to them are their celestial patrons with their names inscribed in Old Church Slavonic

Arkhangelsky sobor

tion: they decided to keep the gold and drowned the boy in the sea. They told the prior that the boy had fled and they never found the treasure. In the meantime, Archangel Michael had rescued the boy from the bottom of the sea and brought him back to the monastery safe and sound. With the boy standing next to him, the prior was able to indict and punish the evil monks. In the scene between the top windows on the southerly wall, Archangel Michael constitutes Moses as the King, illustrating the celestial provenance of earthly power.

Gracious Heaven Icon of Our Lady. 17th century

Closer to the iconostasis on the northerly wall, there is the mural The Miracle at Khony, in which Archangel Michael saves

a Christian temple from the pagans, who were plotting to redirect a mountain stream to destroy it. The Archangel cracked a rock open with his scepter, and the water sank into the crack. The place was then renamed Khony, meaning "hole." Above it is the mural The Vision of King Constantine. According to a legend, Archangel Michael had appeared to Byzantine Emperor Constantine before a battle, proffering a cross bearing the inscription: "with this you shall win." Constantine promised to convert to Christianity, and subsequently defeated his enemies.

The life-size images of nearly all the princes buried here — from Ivan Kalita and Vasily III (more than 60 rulers) — are painted on the wall in front of their tombstones. Each image is individual, but may not be a true portrait since no historical descriptions exist. All are facing the altar, except Dmitry Donskoi, whose image was repainted with this mistake after an 18th century restoration. On the pillars are the images of the Holy Prince Vladimir, St. Alexander Nevsky, the first Russian saints Boris and Gleb, and other princes canonized as saints.

Iconostasis

The 13-meter tall gilded iconostasis rises up to the vaulted ceiling. The lime tree iconostasis was carved by court engravers in 1679–1680. The bottom row consists of old icons that were divested of their gold and silver settings after the 1917 Bolshevik takeover.

To the right of the Holy Doors is the icon of Jesus Christ the King, showing Christ in Byzantine royal vestments. In the 19th century, the image was covered with a silver setting weighing more than 25 kg.

Other sacred objects in the church include an icon of Archangel Michael (late 14th — early 15th centuries) — it's second to the right of the Holy Doors. According to a legend, the icon was painted after the Archangel appeared to Princess Eudokia, the widow of Prince Dmitry Donskoi.

The paintings on the southerly door show a guardian angel bearing a cross, fol-

The westerly wall mural The Day of Judgement

Arkhangelsky sobor

Iconostasis
1. Christ the King wearing imperial robes. 2. Gracious Heaven Icon of Our Lady.
3. Icon of Archangel Michael

lowed by the "Angel of the Wilderness" icon of St. John the Precursor. John the Baptist, who spent most of his life in the wilderness, is shown as a hermit with angel wings. The tomb of Ivan the Terrible, who considered St. John his celestial patron, is behind the icon. The walls of the St. John Chapel are painted with scenes from the life of St. John the Baptist.

In the bottom row near the right edge of the iconostasis is the image of St. Nicholas of Mozhaisk, holding a temple in one hand, symbolizing Mozhaisk, a town near Moscow, and a sword in the other, symbolizing protection.

To the left of the Holy Doors stands the Gracious Heaven icon of Our Lady, a 17th century copy of the original older icon, brought from Smolensk to Moscow in 1391 by Sophia, the daughter of Lithuanian Prince Vitovt, who married Vasily I. The icon came

to Smolensk from Constantinople. To the left is the Icon of the Annunciation of Our Lady of Ustiug, in which Archangel Gabriel announces to Virgin Mary she is going to have a son. This is a 16th century copy of an older icon Ivan the Terrible brought from Novgorod. The original, credited with miraculous powers, is at the Tretyakov Gallery.

On the northerly (Deacon's) door is an image of the First Holy Martyr Archdeacon Stephan. Left of the door stands the icon of St. Basil the Great, one of the founders of the Orthodox Church and namesake of several princes buried in the church. The last image in the same row is a 17th century icon of St. Theodore the Stratelates, a martyr who died for the Christian faith in the 4th century.

The icons in the other rows, painted between 1679 and 1681, bear scenes that were typical for the Gospel, Prophets and Old Testament rows of contemporary iconostases.

Royal Tombs

The tombstones of Russian rulers fill the entire church space, standing by the walls and between the pillars. The tombs were installed in the 1630s under orders from Czar Mikhail Romanov to replace the older, more modest gravestones. Parishioners soon developed the custom of placing their petitions, addressed personally to the Czar, on the tombstones right before those days when the Czar was wont to come here. People also placed icons, candles and plates with food on the tombstones in memory of the dead. The royal gravestones were covered with red and black velvet with small silver icons and gold embroidered inscriptions. On memorial days, these were replaced with richer covers, inlaid

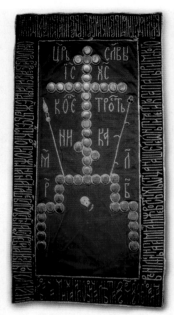

Some of the covers which used to be on the royal tombstones are now on display in the Armory

with gems and pearl thread inscriptions.

The oldest graves are located three in row along the southerly wall. The Holy Prince Dmitry Donskoi, the victor of Khan Mamai, and his brother-in-arms Vladimir the Brave are buried here. In the row nearest to the southerly door is the grave of Prince Ivan Kalita, the early Consolidator of Russia.

Right next to the iconostasis is the grave of Basil II the Dark, whose reign was overshadowed by many grievances. He was temporarily deposed twice, was taken prisoner by the Tartars, and, finally, was blinded in some internecine conflict. Hence his nickname "Dark." Next to his are the graves of his son and grandson — Ivan III and Vasily III. The founder of the modern Kremlin, Ivan III, ended the centuries of Tartar yoke in Russia, married Byzantine princess Sophia Paleolog, and adopted the Byzantine imperial symbol — the double eagle. Vasily III completed the unification of Russia around Moscow.

The grave nearest to the first southerly pillar is the last abode of Ivan III's grandson Dmitry, whom his grandfather crowned with the Hat of Monomakh at the Cathedral of the Assumption in 1498. Later on, in the midst of internal strife within the royal dynasty, Ivan III deposed Dmitry and put him in prison, where he died.

The tombs of Ivan IV the Terrible and his two sons are in the southerly St. John the Precursor Chapel, which is closed to the public. The tombs in the Chapel are covered with cherry colored velvet with yellow crosses. In the corner stands a bronze bust of Ivan the Terrible, whose portrait was reconstructed from his skull by sculptor and anthropologist Mikhail Gerasimov in the 1960s. When the Czar felt his death was near, he hastily took the monastic vows of schema under the name of Jonah — it was believed that all your sins would be absolved

The painting Ivan the Terrible and His Son Ivan by Ilya Repin. According to a legend, Ivan the Terrible hit his son with his staff during a quarrel, but accidentally got him in the temple and killed him

Outermost icons on the southern side of the iconostasis: St. John the Precursor "Angel of the Wilderness" and St. Nicholas of Mozhaisk

Impostor, was buried by the southerly wall of the St. John the Precursor Chapel in 1610. There is evidence that Skopin-Shuisky was poisoned at the feast thrown in celebration of his victory. The first tomb left of the entrance is of Czar Vasily Shuisky, or Vasily IV. The Boyars put him in charge in 1606 after deposing Dmitry I the Impostor. Vasily Shuisky was himself deposed and forced into monasticism in 1610. The provisional Boyar government made a pact with Polish troops, and let them into the Kremlin. Shuisky was imprisoned and died in captivity. After a peace treaty was signed with Poland, Czar Mikhail ordered Shuisky's remains back to Moscow, where they were interred with regal honors at the Cathedral of the Archangel Michael in 1635. Shuisky's grave is next to that of Prince Vladimir Staritsky, Ivan the Terrible's cousin whom the Czar suspected of participation in a conspiracy to oust him. Ivan made Prince Vladimir drink a goblet of poisoned wine.

The first Romanovs, buried in the middle of the Cathedral, by the southeasterly pillar, next to the shrine of the Holy Prince Dmitry, were Czar Mikhail, his son Alexius and grandsons Theodore and Ivan. The last ruler to be buried here was Peter II, who died of smallpox in Moscow right before his own wedding at the age of 15. Peter II's grave is across from the northeasterly pillar.

Lining the northerly and westerly walls are 12 graves of Great Princes and appanage princes. Those who had pledged allegiance to the Prince of Moscow at the Assumption

when you became a monk. Ivan was buried wearing his schema robes. An examination of Ivan the Terrible's skeleton revealed that he was around 180 cm tall and heavy-set. His bones were found to contain an abnormally large quantity of mercury, but this can hardly corroborate the poisoning theory: some medicines were made with mercury in those times.

The remains of Boris Godunov, who died in 1605, were interred next to Czar Feodor for a little while before being removed in 1606 under orders from Dmitry I the Impostor. Godunov's remains were removed secretly through an aperture in the southerly wall of the Chapel, the traces of which can still be discerned. Boris Godunov is now buried at the Holy Trinity & St. Sergius Lavra.

The Russian military leader Mikhail Skopin-Shuisky, who defended Moscow successfully against the troops of Dmitry II the

The tombstones over the graves of Ivan the Terrible and his sons Ivan and Feodor

Arkhangelsky sobor

Tombs of Russian Czars and Princes

1. Czar Ivan the Terrible (1530–1584). His sons, Czarevich Ivan (1554–1581) and Czar Feodor (1557–1598).

2. Prince Vasily II the Dark (1415–1462). Prince Ivan III (1440–1505), the first to self-apply the title of Lord of All Russia. Prince Vasily III (1479–1533). Czarevich Dmitry (1552–1553), Ivan the Terrible's son, who died in his infancy.

3. Prince Ivan Kalita (late 13th century – 1340), the grandson of St. Alexander Nevsky. Prince Simeon the Proud (1317–1353). Prince George of Moscow (1533–1563), Ivan the Terrible's younger brother.

4. Prince Ivan the Red (1326–1359), the son of Ivan Kalita and father of Dmitry Donskoi. Holy Virtuous Prince Dmitry Donskoi (1350–1389). Prince Dmitry Zhilka of Uglich (ca. 1481–1521), the third son of Ivan III and Sophia Paleolog, Appanage Prince of Uglich.

5. Prince Vasily I (1371–1425), Dmitry Donskoi's eldest son. Prince Ivan Junior (before 1473–1490), the son and heir of Ivan III, was nominated his co-ruler, but did not live to become the sole ruler. Prince Dmitry (1483–1509), the son of Ivan Junior and grandson of Ivan III, was the first to have a royal coronation at the Cathedral of the Assumption.

6. Prince Andrew (1327–1353), the younger son of Ivan Kalita and father of Vladimir the Brave. Prince Vladimir the Brave (1353–1410), cousin and brother-in-arms of Dmitry Donskoi in the Battle of Kulikovo. Prince Yuri of Zvenigorod (ca. 1374–1434), Prince Vasily the Cross-Eyed (ca. 1421–1448), Prince Dmitry the Red (ca. 1406 – ca. 1440), Dmitry Donskoi's second son and two grandsons, who took part in an internecine war over the Moscow throne. Prince Andrew of Mozhaisk (1382–1432), one of the younger sons of Dmitry Donskoi. Prince Peter Dmitrovsky (1385–1428), one of the younger sons of Dmitry Donskoi. Prince Ivan the Big (1396–1417), Vasily I's son and heir to the throne, didn't live to succeed his father. Prince Simeon of Kaluga (1487–1518), the fourth son of Ivan III and Sophia Paleolog. Ivan III's brothers: Princes George Dmitrovsky (ca. 1441–1472), Boris

Volotsky (after 1433–1494) and Andrew Junior (ca. 1452–1481). Prince Ivan of Serpukhov (1381–1422), the son of Vladimir the Brave. Prince Afanasy-Yaroslav of Maloyaroslavets (ca. 1388–1426), the son of Vladimir the Brave.

7. Czar Vasily IV Shuisky (1557–1612). Prince Vladimir Staritsky (after 1533–1569); Prince Vasily Staritsky (ca. 1552 – ca. 1574), cousin and nephew of Ivan the Terrible. Prince Andrew Staritsky (1490–1536), the younger brother of Vasily III, was tortured and killed on a false accusation of conspiracy against Elena Glinskaya.

8. Prince George Dmitrovsky (1480–1536), the second son of Ivan III and Sophia Paleolog. Prince Andrew of Radonezh (after 1372–1426), another son of Vladimir the Brave. Prince Andrew of Uglich (1446 – ca. 1494), the third son of Vasily II, died in prison, where he had been thrown by his brother Ivan III.

9. Czar Mikhail Romanov (1596–1645). Czar Alexius (1629–1676). His son Czarevich Alexius (1654–1670) and brother Czarevich Ivan (died in 1639). Mikhail's brother Czarevich Vasily (died in 1639). Alexius' sons Czarevich Dmitry (died in 1650) and Simeon (died in 1669). Czarevich Ilya, Feodor's son (died in 1681). Czarevich Alexander, Peter's son (1691–1692).

10. Czar Feodor (1661–1682). Czar Ivan (1666–1696), Peter I's elder half-brother and co-ruler.

11. Emperor Peter II (1715–1730), Peter I's grandson, Czarevich Alexius' son.

12. Tartar Czarevich Peter (his name before conversion to Christianity was Kudaikul, died in 1509), the husband of Vasily III's sister.

13. Alexander, Czar of Kazan (before conversion: Khan Utemish-Girei, died in 1566).

14. Prince Vasily Borovsky (died in 1483), Vladimir the Brave's grandson. Formerly an aide-de-camp of Vasily II, he fell into disfavor and died in prison.

15. Prince Mikhail Skopin-Shuisky (1586–1610), the military leader who liberated most of the Russian land captured by the troops of Dmitry II the Impostor.

16. The antique shrine of the Holy Prince Mikhail of Chernigov (1195–1246).

17. Shrine of the Hole Czarevich Dmitry (1583–1591).

Layout of the Cathedral of the Archangel Michael

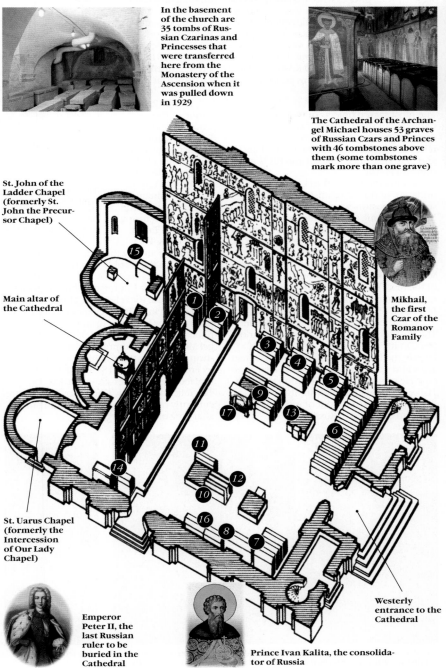

In the basement of the church are 35 tombs of Russian Czarinas and Princesses that were transferred here from the Monastery of the Ascension when it was pulled down in 1929

The Cathedral of the Archangel Michael houses 53 graves of Russian Czars and Princes with 46 tombstones above them (some tombstones mark more than one grave)

St. John of the Ladder Chapel (formerly St. John the Precursor Chapel)

Main altar of the Cathedral

Mikhail, the first Czar of the Romanov Family

St. Uarus Chapel (formerly the Intercession of Our Lady Chapel)

Westerly entrance to the Cathedral

Emperor Peter II, the last Russian ruler to be buried in the Cathedral

Prince Ivan Kalita, the consolidator of Russia

Arkhangelsky sobor

Cathedral during their life were buried by the westerly wall; princes who had fallen into disfavor with the Moscow ruler were buried by the northerly wall. Among the other graves by the westerly wall are the tombs of Appanage Prince Yuri, who took over the throne in Moscow briefly in 1434, but died soon thereafter, and his son Vasily Kosoi (Cross-Eyed), who was blinded by his political rivals.

Sacred Objects

The most sacred objects of worship at the Cathedral of the Archangel Michael are the relics of the Holy Prince Dmitry, and the relics of the Chernigov Miracle-Workers and Martyrs Prince Mikhail and his Boyar subject Feodor.

Dmitry died in 1591 in Uglich at age 8 under mysterious circumstances. A succession of impostors would try to usurp the Moscow throne under Dmitry's name. Dmitry I the Impostor moved into the Kremlin in 1605, and Muscovites recognized him as their Czar. When Dmitry the Impostor was exposed and killed, the newly elected Czar Vasily Shuisky hurriedly brought the remains of the real Dmitry back from Uglich. The remains were declared imperishable and placed on display first at Lobnoe Mesto, then at the Cathedral of the Archangel Michael. The Russian Orthodox Church soon canonized Dmitry as a saint. In 1607, a second Dmitry the Impostor turned up with a great army and set up camp in Tushino near Moscow. He was nicknamed "Tushino thief." In 1610, Prince Mikhail Skopin-Shuisky kicked the impostor's troops out of most places they had captured in Russia.

In 1630, Czar Mikhail ordered a silver shrine made for Dmitry's relics. But Napoleon's soldiers stole the shrine in 1812. The silver shrine lid is on display at the Armory.

The antique shrine of the Chernigov Miracle-Workers stands close to the northwesterly pillar. Mikhail, the Prince of Chernigov, and Boyar Feodor were assassinated by the Tartar Horde in 1246 for refusing to worship Tartar pagan idols. Their

The gold censer from the vestry of the Cathedral of the Archangel Michael is now on display at the Armory

remains are among the oldest relics in Russia. Ivan the Terrible ordered them to Moscow from Chernigov in 1572, and had the eponymous Chernigov Church specially built to house the relics. The church was dismantled in 1770 when a new palace was planned for Catherine II, and the relics were relocated to the Cathedral of the Archangel Michael. The Empress ordered a silver shrine made for them, which was also stolen by French soldiers in 1812, and was later replaced with a silver-plated bronze one. The relics of the Holy Chernigov Martyrs are currently housed in a shrine standing in the altar area of the Cathedral.

The shrine of the Holy Czarevich Dmitry under a canopy (left). The silver lid (right) from his tombstone with an embossed image of the Czarevich is on display at the Armory

Blagoveschensky Sobor
(Cathedral of the Annunciation)

The domestic chapel of the Russian sovereigns is located in the south-western part of the Sobornaya (Cathedral) Square and the west wall joins the Grand Kremlin Palace. It was dedicated in honour of the Annunciation of the Holy Mother of Christ – the symbolism of this celebration can be understood as a blessing for the continuation of humanity.

One of the most famous of the priests in the 16th century was Father Silvestr, mentor to the young Ivan the Terrible, having established the famous Domostroi, Rules for Household Living. The Cathedral's Dean was the czar's confessor, who heard the sovereign's confession and with whom he carried out communion. This tradition survived even when the Imperial Residence was relocated to St. Petersburg. The emperor's and empress' confessor, residing in the new capital, was nonetheless considered the protoierei (arch priest) of the Cathedral of the Annunciation.

The cathedral was constructed in the 15th–16th centuries. The nine-cupolas represent the nine ranks of angels. Beside the main altar of the Cathedral, there was also a side altar of St. Nicholas the Miracle Worker in the southern gallery arranged according to the will of Nicholas I, and four side altars in the corners of the second storey of the Cathedral — The Entrance of the Savior to Jerusalem, the Archangel Gabriel, the Gloryfication of the Holy Mother of Christ and St. George (rededicated in 1822 under the reign of Emperor Alexander I to St. Alexander Nevsky). After the Revolution of 1917, the new

Icon of Our Lady of Don is now in Tretyakov Gallery. Its frame depicting 18 matriarchs (righteous women of the Old Testament) is now bordering the icon of Our Lady of Shuya-Smolensk in the Cathedral

←   **Interior of the Cathedral in the late 19th century**

government no longer needed religion and turned the cathedral into a museum.

At present the Altar of the Annunciation is in use, and services are held in celebration of the Annunciation of the Holy Mother of Christ (7 April). On this day, according to ancient Russian tradition, the Patriarch of Moscow and All the Russia releases white doves from the steps of the Cathedral.

Layout of the Cathedral
The cathedral is actually even smaller than it appears, since on three sides on the inside there is a gallery. Formerly, the church was joined to the Czar's Palace but in the 18th century the entrance was blocked up and the main entrance became the one which is currently used, on the eastern wall. The cupolas above the corners of the Cathedral mark the former altars, which were located on the second storey above the gallery. Access to them was only possible from the side of the Palace along the roof of the gallery. It is possible that such an unusual location saved the altars from ravage in 1812: the French for some reason did not touch the altars and the ancient silver iconostasis. When they left the Kremlin it was discovered that the locks and seals had not been forced or even tampered.

The cathedral's cupolas were first gilded in 1508. Ivan the Terrible has them covered with gold a second time. Patriarch Nikon told the archdeacon Paul of Aleppo — that not only all nine cupolas of the cathedral had been gilded with a fingers width of gold but also the eaves and gutters. However, one must confess that Patriarch Nikon was exaggerating. However, this myth, nonetheless, continued since the Annunciation Cathedral

Blagoveschensky Sobor

cupolas do indeed shine more brightly than others in the Kremlin. The reason for this is that Alexander II in the 1860s had them covered with copper sheets with a heavier coat of gold and in the 1960s they were again gilded with another layer.

Cathedral Frescoes

Through the northern-east entrance to the cathedral the ambassadors of Orthodox countries walked towards the Czar of All the Rus. Above the entrance is an ancient fresco Gloryfication of the Mother of God. Angels, the Three Wise Men, shepherds, the personification of Earth and Desert, saints and representatives of the Human Race gathered to glorify the Mother of God and her son sitting on the throne.

The staircase leading to the porch is so high because beneath the cathedral is a podklet (lower floor) which served as a treasury in the 15ᵗʰ–16ᵗʰ centuries. Nowadays, archaeological finds which have been discovered on Kremlin territory are exhibited here.

On the southern wall of the inner porch one can see a fresco with a biblical theme The Capture of Jericho depicting how the Israelis breached the walls with the sound of the famous horns. Their efforts were helped by the crowd of angels led by Archangel Gabriel. A side chapel dedicated to the Archangel is located above the inner porch. The inner porch leads to the northern gallery, covered with wonderful frescoes, which were recovered at the end of the 19ᵗʰ century and in the 1950s–60s, having been covered over by more recent paintings. The majority of the frescoes date from the time of Ivan the Terrible.

As you enter through the second door, turn around and you'll see above the doorway The Saviour surrounded by angels. Tradition has it that this was painted by the famous icon artist of the 17ᵗʰ century Simon Ushakov.

On the vaults of the northern gallery is the family tree of Jesus Christ, known as Drevo Iesseevo (Stock of Jesse). The fresco, in which there are over two hundred figures,

View of the Cathedral of the Annunciation

1. Chapel of the Archangel Gabriel. 2. Chapel of the Glorification of Our Lady. 3. Chapel of the Entrance of the Savior to Jerusalem. 4. Chapel of St. Alexander Nevsky. 5. Podklet (lower floor) of the Cathedral

Layout of the Cathedral

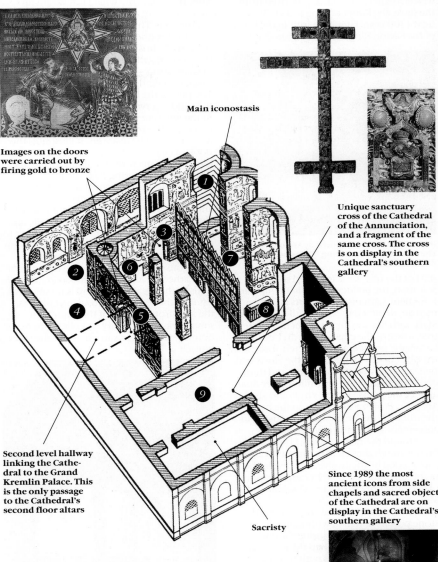

Main iconostasis

Images on the doors were carried out by firing gold to bronze

Unique sanctuary cross of the Cathedral of the Annunciation, and a fragment of the same cross. The cross is on display in the Cathedral's southern gallery

Second level hallway linking the Cathedral to the Grand Kremlin Palace. This is the only passage to the Cathedral's second floor altars

Since 1989 the most ancient icons from side chapels and sacred objects of the Cathedral are on display in the Cathedral's southern gallery

Sacristy

1. Main entrance
2. Northern gallery
3. Northern portal
4. Western gallery
5. Western portal
6. Staircase to the second level gallery
7. Main altar
8. Silver shrine with the relics of some 50 saints
9. Southern gallery

Blagoveschensky Sobor

begins at the entrance and finishes in the western gallery. The name is derived from the Jesse, the father of King David. Whose seed 1100 years later bore fruit in the form of the Savior. King David is pictured at the

Image of The Savior painted by Simon Ushakov. The Stock of Jesse painting begins here on the vaults of the gallery

start of the tree. He is followed by King Solomon, the builder of the first temple in Jerusalem. Other Israeli leaders and wise men are depicted right up until the Mother Mary with her son. In the branches of the tree, towards the edges of the arches and pilasters the prophets are depicted, foretelling the birth of Christ, including the Sibyls and twelve Greek and Roman poets and thinkers. Among them are the philosopher Anaxagoras, the poets Homer, Virgil, and also Aristotle, Ptolemy and Plato. In the hands of the thinkers are scrolls with aphorisms, in agreement with Christian thought.

Around the next corner of the gallery on the arches there is a picture of the Savior surrounded by the twelve apostles. In the branches of the tree, the Byzantine emperors and the princes of Kiev, Vladimir and Moscow are depicted.

Particularly beautiful are the carved stone portals of Italian workmanship, adorning the entrances inside the church. Today they look richer than the iconostasis, missing the silver frames with pearls and precious stones. On the bronze doors of the northern portal, near the entrance there are scenes of the prophecy about Christ and the Virgin Mary. The images on the unique gate were carried out by firing gold to bronze.

On the right from the gate there is scene from the Old Testament The Miracle of Jonah the Prophet, which was very popular among the Rus. St. Jonah did not listen to

God and for this was swallowed by a whale. After three days the whale threw him up onto the shore and Jonah followed God's instructions. This story was always understood as prophesizing the death and resurrection of Christ. On the wall at the end of the western gallery it is possible to see Deeds of Confession — depictions of monks, who torment their flesh in every possible way. The plot of the book written by St. John of the Ladder served as the basis for this scene. At the juncture with the western wall there is one of the earliest frescoes, The Holy Trinity, discovered by restorers. It illustrates the Book of Genesis: Abraham and Sarah take into their home three travelling angels and overhear them during their meal.

Let us look at the decoration of the church, in which the Russian czars prayed and made confession. As a rule they did this alone. The Czarina and Czarevich (wife and crown prince of the Czar) were forbidden to enter the church while the Czar was praying or confessing. For them special galleries were constructed above the western part of the Cathedral. A staircase hidden in the wall leads to these galleries. There is no solea (a rising in the floor which usually separates the altar from the rest of the church), it simply was unnecessary in a place where the holy mysteries were carried out by the Czar himself.

Murals of the inner porch

Door portals by Italian masters were made in the 16th century

The scenes on the walls are the remains of an ancient fresco dating to the 16th–17th centuries. In order to clean them, restorers removed up to 5–6 layers of more recent frescoes. Among the frescoes of the cathedral there are many stories to compel repentance: a vision of the Apocalypse, scenes from the Day of Judgement and the suffering of the sinful.

On the columns are depictions of great princes: Prince St. Vladimir, Vladimir Monomakh, St. Alexander Nevsky, Ivan Kalita and St. Dmitry Donskoy. As in the Cathedral of the Arkhangel Michael, they are depicted with halos, including those who have not been canonized.

The floor of the church is made of uneven squares from extremely rare jasper. According to legend, these tiles were taken from Uspensky Sobor (Cathedral of the Assumption) in Veliky (Great) Rostov during the time of Ivan the Terrible.

The scriptures relate two important dates in the cathedral's history on the left and right columns nearest to the iconostasis. The first is the construction of the church in 1489 under Ivan III. The second is the renovation of the church which occurred in 1697 under Peter the Great.

The Iconostasis and Relics

One of the oldest iconostases in Russia is located in the cathedral. It appears to be almost the same today as it was in 1812 after the French invasion. All the silver ornaments on the icons were removed, all that remains is the frame on the icon The Mother of Christ on the left from the Holy Doors. The actual iconostasis with the low panelling in the shape of large medallions with inscriptions was made in the second half of the 19th century from gilded bronze with enamel. In the iconostasis ancient icons from the 14th–16th centuries have been preserved.

The icons of the upper two rows of the iconostasis portraying the Patriarch's and the prophets of the Old Testament at their full height are the oldest of this kind.

More honored are the icons, which as ever, are located in the lower row. The most ancient is the icon The All Merciful Savior, which stands first to the right from the Holy Doors. A later inscription on the icon says that it was painted in 1337 by a certain "Sinful Mikhail", working in the court of the Great Prince Ivan Kalita. Later the icon was given to the Archbishop of Novgorod Moisei. In 1570, Ivan the Terrible, believing a false denunciation, massacred the inhabitants of Novgorod. Soldiers of the Czar's oprichnina (the special political-administrative body which Ivan the Terrible established to run his own lands directly) robbed the churches and monasteries of Novgorod. Many sacred relics were carried back to Moscow. Amongst the items taken

Icon of the Annunciation (17th century)

away was this picture. The Savior is pointing out the words: Judge not lest thee be judged. Notice that the surviving painting preserved on the icon dates to the time of Ivan the Terrible.

On the left hand side from the Holy Doors is located the icon of the Mother of God of Shuya-Smolensk. The icon became famous for the redemption of the citizens in the town of Shuya who were saved from the plague in 1654–1655. The unusual frame, which was preserved from an earlier icon was made towards the end of the 17th century. A popular scene for Western European canvases in the 18th century was the 18 Wise

women of the Old Testament. Among them is Eve as the progenetrix of the human race (in the centre of the top); Ruth, the great grandmother of Isaiah, who has been mentioned above; Anne, the mother of the prophet Samuel and others.

To the right of The All Merciful Savior is the icon of the Annunciation of Ustyug (17th century). The 24 stamps on the frame of the icon represent acathistus to the Mother of Christ.

Beyond the Annunciation icon in the lower row of the iconostasis of the Cathedral of the Annunciation the icon of the patron saint of the current sovereign used

Main iconostasis of the Cathedral of the Annunciation

1. Icon of the All Merciful Savior (14th–16th century). 2. Icon of Our Lady of Shuya-Smolensk (17th century). 3. Icon of the Annunciation of Ustyug (17th century). 4. Icon of St. John the Baptist, apostle St. Peter and St. Alexius, Man of God (1680s). 5. Icon of The Savior on the Throne (17th century)

to be placed. From the time of Czars Ivan and Peter I the icon of St. John the Baptist and the apostle St. Peter has been placed here. In the middle of the 18th century the image of St. Alexius, Man of God, has been painted on it. After the southern gate in the lower row of the iconostasis stands the icon of the Savior of Smolensk dating to the middle of the 16th century. To the right of it on the southern wall is located an icon which is known as The Four Parts icon (1540–1550). The icon illustrates several theological texts, however the pictures are highly unusual for Orthodox believers and this became a reason for the revolt in icon painting leading to new innovations. Several researchers suggest that among the people in the icon (to the left and bottom) are depicted the young Czar, Ivan the Terrible and his wife, Czarina Anastasia.

Icon of Glorification of Our Lady from the Chapel of the same dedication

Other icons from the left side of the iconostasis, beyond the Shuisky-Smolensky image of the Mother of Christ are: one more Savior on the Throne, The Mother of Christ and an icon of St. Nicholas with the scenes. of his life. They date to the 16th–18th centuries.

Shrine and former Cathedral Sacristy

Beyond the iconostasis from the southern side of the building is one of the largest relics at the Kremlin, a large, silver shrine. In it are preserved relics of nearly fifty saints (John the Baptist, the Apostle Andrew the First Called, George the Victorious, John, bishop of Constantinople and many others). These relics were sent from the 15 century onwards as gifts to the Russian czars from Greece. By 1680 under Czar Feodor they numbered 138 relics. Several were poorly looked after, and for that reason Patriarch Ioakim gave permission to distribute some of them amongst the monasteries and churches. The remaining part, 107 relics, were preserved as before in individual cases. In 1894, Peter Smirnov, a Moscow merchant and founder of the famous vodka company, paid for the manufacture of a silver shrine (Smirnov at that time was a starosta (elder) of court cathedrals). In Soviet times, some of these relics were given to the church, and they were distributed among Moscow churches.

The Southern Gallery

(The former side altar of St. Nicholas the Miracle Worker)

The altar arranged in 1836 to the orders of Nicholas I has not been preserved. Now in its place is the display for the cathedral's icons. The most ancient icons of the main and side altars of the cathedral date to the 14–16 centuries and are protected by windows. Here is an entire iconostasis from the Chapel of the Archangel Gabriel. In it is a copy of the miraculous Icon of Our Lady of Smolensk which at one stage was the main relic of the Cathedral. According to legend, the original icon was painted by the evangelist Luka, and was later brought to Uspensky Sobor (Cathedral of Assumption) of Smolensk by Prince Vladimir Monomakh and through its wonders helped defend the city from Tartar attack. At the beginning of the 15th century, the image was taken to Moscow and in 1456 Czar Vasily II the Dark returned it to Smolensk at the request of its citizens.

Silver shrine for holy relics was made in 19th century

Ivan the Great Bell Tower

In the middle of the Kremlin towers the golden-domed pillar of the Ivan (John) the Great Bell Tower with two smaller belfries adjacent from the north. The tower's name implies that it had once housed St. John's Church, and that it used to be the tallest building in Moscow.

The Tower goes back to 1329, when Ivan Kalita ordered a small St. John's Church built in the Kremlin. In 1505–1508, the dilapidated church building was replaced with a pillar-like bell tower around 60 m tall, built by the Italian architect Bon Friazin to the order of Ivan III. The old church continued divine services in the basement of the new building, sized only 25 square meters with walls as thick as 5 m.

Boris Godunov, who became Czar in 1598, ordered the bell tower built up in aggrandizement of what he thought was the start of the Godunov royal family line. But Godunov's project had yet another reason. Muscovites were starving, so the Czar wanted to give people new jobs and take their minds away from hardship and possible revolt. The tower was built up to 81 meters. Under the dome, a three-line inscription was made listing the names and titles of Boris Godunov, his son Feodor, and the date the tower was built up.

Common townsfolk believed the cross on top of the tower was pure gold. Napoleon ordered it taken down in 1812. Legend has it he wanted to take the cross to France and put it up on top of Les Invalides in Paris. But while the French soldiers were taking

St. John of the Ladder spiritual "guidebook" had 30 chapters, or "steps" of the stairway towards spiritual perfection and Paradise

the cross down, the ropes broke and it fell down and broke to pieces. It turned out the cross was covered with gilded copper plates that only looked like gold.

In the 16th and 17th centuries, Ivanovskaya (St. John's) Square — the plaza in front of the Tower — was occupied by government ministry buildings. This was where the Czar's edicts were read out. There was an office in the square, which was a prototype of an early notary's office, where all sorts of petitions were crafted for people for a fee.

Public whippings were also held here: this was the typical punishment for bribery, embezzlement or fraud. Thieves were placed in the middle of the square for public humiliation, and the property they had stolen or tried to steal was hanged around their neck. This could be both valuables and minor items such as dried fish, for instance. From 1685 on, public punishments were meted out in Red Square.

For many decades the bell tower was also the main watchtower in the Kremlin, and later also a fire tower. During the coronation of Nicholas II in 1896, the bell tower was electrically illuminated. Ivan the Great towered like a giant candle above the city.

The bell tower was open to the public before 1917. Its entrance was also the entrance to the church inside. There were two observatories upstairs, one in the middle, right above the lower set of bells, the other above the top bells. 329 steps led to the top of the tower, but the arduous climb was rewarded with a panoramic view of Moscow and its suburbs. On a sunny day, one could see as far as 40 km out from the tower.

← **The three rows of gold letters under the belfry dome read: "With the blessing of the Holy Trinity, under the orders of Our Great Lord, Czar and Great Prince Boris Feodorovich, the Ruler of Russia, and His Son Feodor Borisovich, the Virtuous Great Prince of Russia, this church was built and gilded the second year of their reign, the year 108 (1600)"**

Assumption Belfry

Petrok Maly, the Italian architect who built the Kitai-Gorod wall in Moscow, started construction on the Church of the Resurrection, later

Ivan the Great Bell Tower

renamed Church of the Nativity, next to the Ivan the Great Tower in 1532. Decades later the church was converted to a belfry for large bells, known today as the Assumption Belfry after its main bell — the Assumption Bell.

The steep stone stairway leading to the church entrance on the outside was originally built in 1552, when Ivan the Terrible was Czar. Emperor Paul I ordered the architect Matvei Kazakov to dismantle the stairway to make room for a new corps de guard. In 1852, the stairway was restored "in the old Russian style" by Konstantin Ton, the architect of the Church of Christ the Savior. The stairway is currently closed.

Philaret Annex
The building with a hipped roof next to the Assumption Belfry is the Philaret Annex, named in honor of Patriarch Philaret. In 1624, when Philaret, the father of Czar Mikhail, returned after captivity in Poland,

he ordered this structure built to celebrate his release.

Napoleon ordered the Ivan the Great Bell Tower destroyed in 1812. The explosion destroyed the belfry and the annex, but the larger parts survived and were used in 1815 to restore the whole complex by a group of architects, including Domenico Gilardi, Luigi Rusca and Ivan Yegotov. The bell tower, a brick building with white stone slabs in the foundation and basement, survived the explosion with a just a crack at the top. Its foundation being only 5 meters deep, the testifies to the superior craft of its architects and builders.

The Bells of Ivan the Great Tower
Ivan the Great is the belfry for all major churches on the Kremlin compound. The Cathedral of the Assumption, Archangel Michael and Annunciation have no belfries of their own. When the bells of Ivan the

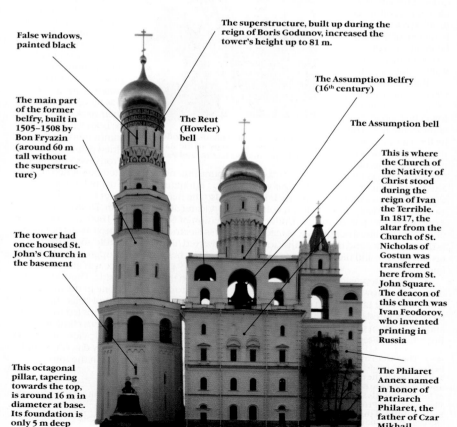

False windows, painted black

The superstructure, built up during the reign of Boris Godunov, increased the tower's height up to 81 m.

The main part of the former belfry, built in 1505–1508 by Bon Fryazin (around 60 m tall without the superstructure)

The Reut (Howler) bell

The Assumption Belfry (16th century)

The Assumption bell

The tower had once housed St. John's Church in the basement

This is where the Church of the Nativity of Christ stood during the reign of Ivan the Terrible. In 1817, the altar from the Church of St. Nicholas of Gostun was transferred here from St. John Square. The deacon of this church was Ivan Feodorov, who invented printing in Russia

This octagonal pillar, tapering towards the top, is around 16 m in diameter at base. Its foundation is only 5 m deep

The Philaret Annex named in honor of Patriarch Philaret, the father of Czar Mikhail

Great began tolling, this triggered chimes all over Moscow. The unwritten custom was initiated by Metropolitan Plato in the 18th century. The Patriarch strictly forbade any church in Moscow to toll ahead of the Great Assumption Bell on any occasion. Incepting in the Kremlin, festive chimes rolled out like waves, sweeping Moscow, gaining strength, evolving into an awe-inspiring bell symphony. The largest Assumption bell, weighing 4,000 poods or upwards of 65.5 tons, hanging in the central vault of the Assumption Belfry, was cast in 1817–1819 by bell founder Yakov Zavialov, who was aged 90 at the time, and cannon founder Rusinov, who used parts of an older bell that had broken when Napoleon tried to blow up the belfry in 1812.

Another much-worshipped icon from the Church of St. Nicholas of Gostun, a carved icon also known as St. Nicholas of Mozhaisk, is currently part of the early Russian sculpture exposition at the Church of the Deposition of the Robe of the Holy Virgin.

The craftsmen repeated the original images of the Savior and Our Lady, as well as Czars Alexius and Peter I on the new bell, adding the images of Alexander I and members of the royal family. At the bottom of the bell there is a five-line text about how Napoleon's troops were defeated and how the bell was cast.

The Reut bell in the next vault was cast in 1622 under orders from Patriarch Philaret by Andrei Chokhov, the same craftsman who cast the Czar Cannon. The exact weight of the bell is not known to this day. Some sources claim it's 1,200 poods (19.6 tons); others name 2,000 poods (32.6 tons). The Reut ("Revun" or "Howler" in the common parlance) has a very low-pitched sound, like a subwoofer to the other bells. The bell fell down in the 1812 explosion, but was restored and never lost its sound quality.

When the Kremlin bells tolled for the enthronement of Alexander II in 1855, the bell fell again, crushing the belfry vaults. A few sextons were killed.

This was viewed as a bad omen for the emperor. Indeed, Alexander II survived five attempts on his life before being assassinated by Narodnaya Volya (People's Will) terrorists.

The Semisotnyi (or Seven Hundred) Bell, cast in 1704, hangs in the Philaret Annex. Its name comes from its weight, which is 798 poods or 13 tons. It was cast by Ivan Motorin, the creator of the Czar Bell. The bell tolled to announce the Lent, when all the other bells remained silent.

There are six 17th–18th century bells in the lower level of Ivan the Great: Medved ("Bear"), Lebed ("Swan"), Novgorodskiy, Shirokiy ("Wide"), Slobodskoi and Rostovskiy. There are 10 more bells in the middle rung, dating back to the 16th and 17th centuries, and another three smaller 17th century bells at the top.

All the bells have been recently tested, and those of them that still work have been used during divine services at the Kremlin. In the past, simultaneous chiming of all Ivan the Great bells was a memorable, jubilant occasion for all Muscovites.

The Assumption bell tolled only on great holidays and to announce events of exceptional significance

Czar Bell

Another Kremlin curio, the Czar Bell, stands on a granite pedestal next to the Ivan the Great Bell Tower. It is the largest church bell in the world, and many think that's why it is called "Czar Bell." But in fact, any bell with the image of a Czar was called "Czar Bell" in Russia at the time.

The Czar Bell weighs about 200 tons. It is 6.14 m tall with a girth of 6.6 m and walls 61 cm thick. The bell fragment next to it weighs about 11.5 tons.

On the two opposite sides of the bell, there are molded images of Czar Alexius I and Empress Anna. Above them, in circular medallions, are the images of Christ, Virgin Mary, the Evangelists, and Moscow Metropolitans canonized as saints. On the sides of the bell, one finds detailed information about how the bell was created, surrounded by a fascinating bas-relief ornament with angel figures in 18th century style.

One of the inscriptions informs us that the bell was cast during the reign of Empress Anna, in the year 7241 of the Creation, or 1733 A.D., and weighs 10,000 poods (163 tons). Both pieces of information are incorrect. The bell was made in 1735, and weighs 2000 poods more than claimed. This discrepancy is explained by the fact that the inscription had been carved into the original casting mold, but the first casting failed. The bell was recast again two years later and it came out heavier, but its "birth certificate" remained the same.

The Czar Bell was made from tin bronze — the kind routinely used to make bells — with some admixtures and other metals. Alloy ingredients: copper: >170 tons (ca. 85%); tin: ca. 26.5 t (>13%); sulfur: 2.5 t (>1%), zinc, arsenic and other admixtures (gold and silver): ca. 2 t (1%)

On the pedestal, the inscription claims that the bell was stored in the ground for 103 years, and was installed here on 4 August 1836 under the orders of Nicholas I. The same inscription also repeats the incorrect information regarding the year when the bell was cast.

History

In 1654, when Alexius I was Czar, Patriarch Nikon ordered a very large bell cast, which would become the predecessor of the Czar Bell. The bell, also called "Czar Bell" or the Great Assumption Bell, weighed 8000 poods (upwards of 130 tons). According to some records, the bell bore the images of Alexius I and the Patriarch himself. Anecdotal evidence suggests that the bell was cast from the scraps of an even older bell, dating back to the reign of Boris Godunov, destroyed by fire. Olearius, a foreign traveler, wrote about the older bell, claiming that in 1611, it hung in a wooden tower around 5 m tall, and it took 24 people to rock its tongue in order to make it toll. The bell tolled at major holidays, and to welcome foreign ambassadors. One of the fires destroyed the bell tower, and the bell fell down and broke.

The newer bell also fell down and broke in the Kremlin fire of 19 June 1700.

The giant fragments lay scattered near Ivan the Great Bell Tower for thirty years, amazing all visitors. When Anna, Peter I's

1. The sphere with a golden cross is the Orb, one of the symbols of royal power.
2. The names of the founders who cast the bell in 1735: Ivan and Mikhail Motorin.
3. Authors of the molded artwork: sculptor: Feodor Medvedev; engravers: Vasily Kobelev and others.
4. Images of Czars from the Romanov Family.
5. Images of the Saints.
6. The 11.5 ton fragment that broke off in the fire.
7. The octahedral pedestal was designed by Auguste Montferrand in 1836.
8. The 5 meter tongue inside the Czar Bell was probably inherited from its predecessor.

View of Czar Bell in the 19th century. Beyond the Bell are the Maly (Small) Palace and the Church of St. Alexius, demolished after the 1917 Revolution

niece, was crowned in 1730, she immediately ordered the bell restored. In her edict of 26 June 1730, she bluntly rounded the weight of the future bell up to 10,000 poods (around 164 tons). No bells of such magnitude had ever been cast before.

The project was commissioned to the French architect and academic Germaine, who had grave doubts about it, but went ahead and made the drawings. A dedicated small foundry had to be built in one of the courtyards between the Chudov Monastery and the Ivan the Great Bell Tower. A pit 10 m deep and 10 m across was dug next to the furnaces.

The first casting failed, but founder Ivan Motorin kept his hopes up. He made his own drawings, adding another 2000 poods to the weight, but unexpectedly died. His son Mikhail performed the casting in November 1735.

Rumor had it that some pious people threw gold and silver into the melted metal, including their crosses. The bell stayed in the pit, standing on a grated support, while engravers from St. Petersburg worked on the decorations. The bell turned out larger and more expensive than any other bell before or after.

On Trinity Day, 29 May 1737, Moscow was swept by one its strongest fires, known to historians as "The Trinity Fire." The wooden roof above the casting pit caught on fire, and burning logs began falling on the bell. Everyone hurriedly started pouring water on the metal, already red-hot. When they put out the fire, it was revealed that the bell now had numerous cracks, and a 11.5 ton fragment had fallen off.

The Czar Bell stayed in its pit for another hundred years or so before Emperor Nicholas I ordered it lifted up to a pedestal in 1835. There were plans to build a new, larger Imperial Palace, and a giant pit next to it would look embarrassing. The project was committed to the celebrated architect Auguste Montferrand, who had already inspected the bell when he first arrived in Russia in 1819. By that time, Montferrand had built St. Isaac's Cathedral and the Alexander Column in St. Petersburg. Two attempts were made to lift up the bell, and the second one was successful. On 23 July 1836, it took exactly 42 minutes and 33 seconds to lift the bell up along an inclined board deck to the granite pedestal where it has remained since.

The 5 meter tongue inside the Czar Bell

Czar Cannon

The Czar Cannon stands close to the Czar Bell. The information on its bronze barrel says that the cannon weighs 2400 poods, or nearly 39.5 tons; its barrel is 5.34 m long, 120 cm in diameter, and 890 mm in caliber; the walls are approx. 15 cm thick.

Most of the images and inscriptions on the cannon cannot be seen from the ground. On the right side of the barrel, there is an image of Feodor I on horseback, wearing his royal coronet. The inscription reads: "By the Grace of God, Czar and Great Prince Feodor Johannovich, Ruler and Monarch," followed by another inscription, pertaining to whoever ordered the cannon made (in this case, the Czar did): "By the order of the Virtuous and Christ-loving Czar and Great Prince Feodor Johannovich, the Ruler and Monarch of the Greater Russia, and his Devout and Christ-loving Czarina and Great Princess Irina".

On the left side, another inscription informs us that the cannon was cast in the year 7094 of the Creation, or 1586 A.D., the third year of the reign of Czar Feodor I, by cannon founder Andrei Chokhov. All this relates to the barrel only. The gun carriage on wheels, adorned with a lion head and ornament, was made two and a half centuries later: in 1835. The carriage weighs around 34.5 tons. The barrel is real bronze, but the carriage is cast iron, painted to look like bronze.

History

The Czar Cannon was built to "amaze the common folk and inspire awe in the Tartars," who were frequent guests in Moscow, according to a historian. The idea belonged to Boris Godunov, Czar Feodor I's brother-in-law, who ran the country de facto. Cast at the cannon foundry that stood on the Neglinnaya River, the cannon was designed to fire case shots, which consisted of small rocks at the time.

As Godunov had wanted, the cannon was placed next to the Lobnoe Mesto in front of the Cathedral of the Intercession of Our Lady in Red Square, where it could best exemplify the military might of Russia, and symbolically guard the Cathedral of the Intercession of Our Lady and the Spasskie Gate.

Boris Godunov's project flattered his fellow countrymen, who could now proudly say that the largest cannon in the world stood in Moscow's Red Square. On the other hand, it was a clever publicity stunt for Godunov himself.

At the end of the 19th century, the Czar Cannon stood next to the old Kremlin barracks with heaps of small cannonballs in front of it.

1. Czar Feodor on horseback.
2. The inscription saying the cannon was cast in 1586 by cannon founder Andrei Chokhov.

3. The iron cannon carriage was designed by Alexander Briullov and manufactured in 1835.

**View of the Czar Cannon today. The four giant hollow cannonballs were cast
in St. Petersburg in the 19th century; each weighs around 1 ton.**

It is not known where the cannon was in the 17th century. In most likelihood, it had been relegated to the Kremlin backyards, where the new rulers, the Romanov Family, removed all reminders of Boris Godunov. The cannon came into limelight again in the early 1700s, when Peter I put it on display among other historical cannons in his new Arsenal.

In 1812, half of the Arsenal building was blown up by the French and the original wooden carriage of the Czar Cannon burned down.

In 1835, Nicholas I ordered historical Russian cannons to go on display outside the Kremlin barracks, and trophy cannons captured from various enemies, arranged in a row in front of the Arsenal. The Czar Cannon, and the Kremlin's longest ever cannon, called "Unicorn," took a place of prominence at the corner of Senate Plaza.

The carriages were designed by the architect Alexander Briullov, the brother of Karl Briullov the artist. The carriages were manufactured at the shipyard in St. Petersburg. Placed on a carriage again, the Czar Cannon looked as majestic and imposing as ever.

The Grand Kremlin Palace

The Kremlin has been the stronghold of power in Russia from day one. The people who ran the country lived in their royal and princely chambers inside. The life inside the Kremlin was so closely tied to Russia's history and what "The Kremlin" stands for, the story of those palaces has to be told, even through access to them may be denied to the general public. Let's take a quick look at their past and present.

Ivan Kalita made sure his princely palace took the pride of place at the Kremlin, standing atop Borovitsky Hill, overlooking the river. It was originally modest and built in wood. It was not nearly roomy enough for Ivan III, who ordered his Italian architects, who had already impressed him with the Granovitaya Chamber, to build a stone palace for him in 1492.

Ivan the Terrible continued to add more wooden structures to his palace.

The main (southerly) façade of the Grand Kremlin Palace with carved white stone decorations

The nucleus of the palace in those times was its Golden Throne Room, which is now St. George Room.

Boris Godunov had his wooden palace built, literally, on the roof of an existing stone building, so the royal family found themselves living in the tallest building around. Godunov had even more grandiose projects in mind, but his sudden death put them all to rest.

Empress Elizabeth ordered Godunov's shabby chambers remodeled, but her new palace turned out somehow too ornate and less than comfortable to live in, so Catherine II stayed in the houses of various court officials whenever she came to Moscow. Alexander I tried to straighten out the royal abode and rebuild it after the Napoleonic fire. In 1817, new wooden walls were quickly built on the old foundation, walled in with brickwork on either side. It was poorly constructed, and the emperor knew it.

Nicholas I, who loved Moscow and the Kremlin more than his predecessors did, undertook to set things straight once and for all. Nicholas commissioned his new palace to Konstantin Ton, already a celebrated architect who had done good by the emperor with his Church of Christ the Savior. Both those buildings were to symbolize the triumph of the Russian national idea.

The new imperial residence, dubbed Grand Kremlin Palace, took a decade to build but looked good next to the older Kremlin landmarks.

We all know what the front façade of the palace looks like: it's a widely advertised symbol of Moscow and the Russian state.

The palace was built in 1838–1849. Its main, riverside façade stretches for 125 m from east to west. The building is around 50 m tall with dome and flagstaff. The palace is linked to the Terem Palace in the north, adjacent to the Granovitaya Chamber in the east, and the Armory in the west. The building stands on some 3.5 hectares of land.

It was a challenging task for the architect. Nicholas I, who was a devout Russophile, defined the style of the palace as "old Russian." While this concept would agree with the surrounding landmarks, the new palace — intended as a venue for massive, sprawling government functions — had to be a structure of such magnitude that it would be completely incompatible with the old Russian architectural tradition. Ton found a solution. He used "national color" in the façade décor, framing the windows with white stone carved ornaments. The gala rooms on the second floor got two rows of windows each, redolent of the traditional

← One of Moscow's signature views: the Kremlin with its fortress, palaces and churches

Terem with small windows. That's why the two-story palace looks like it has three stories. But Ton's interiors were a riot of imperial extravagance — eclectic, luxurious and jam-packed with priceless finishing materials, a feast for the eye.

The Soviet era spared the building, but some major changes were nevertheless made as some rooms in the palace were used for massive political functions.

In the 1990s, the palace's façade and two main rooms were restored to their original, pre-1917 look. The Soviet national emblem and the letters CCCP (USSR) over the main entrance were replaced with five double eagles with the emblems of the old Russian kingdoms and regions above them: St. Petersburg, Kazan, Moscow, Poland, and others.

They say the palace has some 700 rooms, but our imaginary tour will only

Konstantin Ton, architect of the Grand Kremlin Palace, the Armory and the Church of Christ the Savior (1794–1881)

take in the most remarkable of them, such as the celebrated gala rooms named after the highest Russian national awards: the Orders of St. Vladimir, St. George, St. Alexander, St. Andrew and St. Catherine.

Finishing and decorative materials for the palace came from all parts of the Russian Empire. The broad main staircase with 58 steps and five landings, made from Revel stone (Revel was the old name for Tallinn), leads to the second floor, but before we climb the stairs, let's take a left from the hall to the so-called "Private Half" — the emperor's chambers. The emperor and his family would stay here when visiting Moscow from the new capital, St. Petersburg, but most of the time these rooms stood empty, and there was no one around to admire their gem-incrusted furniture, crystal chandeliers, porcelain standard lamps, malachite

Empress's Drawing Room in the Private Wing of the Grand Kremlin Palace

Joseph Stalin toasting the participants of the 1945 Victory Parade in St. George's Hall

The Grand Kremlin Palace

Church of Christ the Savior and the Moskva River. The walls in the study are partially finished in ash wood, and partially upholstered with green fabric. Six paintings on the walls depict scenes from the 1812 Napoleonic War. It's been a long time since anyone used this study. We can now return to the hall and climb the central staircase to the main rooms on the second floor. Directly ahead lies

pilasters, and bronze mantelpiece clocks. Most of this luxury was created by Russian artists and craftsmen.

Walking by the dining room, drawing room, empresses' office, the boudoir, the bedroom and the reception room, we get to the emperor's study in the corner of the building with a breathtaking view of the

the lobby of the main hall. The entrance is lined with two giant crystal vases. The door is five meters tall, made from solid walnut planks without any glue or nails. A painting by Ilya Repin used to hang here, showing Alexander III talking to a delegation of peasant elders. In the 1950s, it was replaced with a painting of Lenin making a speech at the

Layout of the palace complex, early 1900s

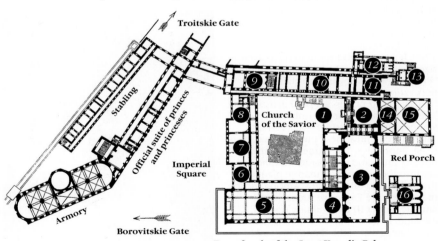

Front façade of the Great Kremlin Palace

1. Boyar landing
2. St. Vladimir Hall
3. St. George Hall
4. St. Alexander Hall
5. St. Andrew Hall
6. Cavalry Guard Hall
7. St. Catherine Hall
8. Empress's official suite
9. Church of the Nativity of God's Mother
10. Terem Palace
11. Czarina's Gold Chamber
12. Palace churches
13. Church of the Deposition of the Robe
14. Sacred Anteroom
15. Granovitaya Chamber
16. Cathedral of the Annunciation

St. George the Victorious fireplace and clock in St. George Hall

3rd Komsomol (Young Communist League) Congress. These days, the painting in the lobby is Whoever Comes to Us with a Sword, Will Die by Sword by Sergei Prisekin.

From the lobby, we enter the most celebrated room in the palace — St. George Hall, which looks exactly the same it did a hundred years ago. The room was named after the military order of St. George the Victorious, established by Catherine II in 1769. It is the largest room in the palace, sized 1250 sq. m with ceilings 17.5 m high. "Progressive" critics used to claim the decorations in this and other main rooms "betray a pretentious, yet poor artistic taste. Their flashy splendor can only impress an uncultured Philistine." Well, call us "uncultured Philistines," but what we see is really impressive. The names of celebrated military units and St. George chevaliers are inscribed in gold on marble plaques in the niches and on the walls. Among those mentioned are Emperors Alexander II and Alexander III and military leaders Alexander Suvorov and Mikhail Kutuzov. New names were added until the end of the 19th century. The 18 columns (nine on either side) are topped with marble female figures with shields bearing the emblems of lands and regions, symbolizing Russia's military victories and lands annexed by Russia over five centuries, from Perm in 1472 to Armenia in 1828, including Ukraine. The bronze mantelpiece clock by

the wall shows St. George on horseback. The clock at the opposite wall is a miniature replica of the monument to Minin and Pozharsky in Red Square. The giant bronze chandeliers are reflected in the parquet, carefully assembled from different kinds of timber — a real piece of art, made from the drawings by art academic Fiodor Solntsev in the 19th century.

Every room was assigned its own role during palace functions in the 19th century. In St. George Room, the emperor would be greeted by Moscow officials, noblemen and honorary citizens. In 1945, a gala reception was held here to celebrate the Soviet Union's victory in WWII after the Victory Parade in Red Square.

The vast wall mirrors in St. Alexander Hall reflect the Moskva River and a panoramic view of the city beyond. This room is dedicated to the Order of St. Alexander Nevsky, established by Catherine I in 1725. The gold decorations on the ceiling and in the arches are bas-reliefs of the order with the letters "S.A.", which stand for Sanctus Alexander, or St. Alexander. The six oblong paintings, three each above on either side of the door illustrate the highlights from the life of Alexander Nevsky, including the 1242 Battle of the Ice and his refusal to worship pagan idols in the Horde. The bas-relief

Inside St. Alexander Hall

above the door shows the prince as a warrior on one side, and as a monk and hermit on the other, symbolizing his earthly and celestial glory. In this room, the emperor would be greeted by Moscow's best ladies. Today, members of the State Council hold their meetings in St. Alexander Hall.

In 1933-1934, St. Alexander Hall was merged with the neighboring St. Andrew Hall for the 17th Communist Party Congress, resulting in an eerily long room dubbed Convention Room, where the Party

The Romanovs' Imperial Symbol on the easterly wall of St. Alexander Hall

and its Supreme Soviet would hold their meetings. A 10-meter marble statue of Lenin was placed inside the niche that had previously housed the emperor's throne. This is where the national sovereignty of Russia was proclaimed on 12 June 1990, starting a new public holiday. The reinstatement of Russian statehood and symbolism called for some changes in palace interiors. Both

rooms were fully restored in 1995–1999.

St. Andrew Hall was named after the first Russian military order: the Order of the Holy Apostle Andrew the First Called, founded by Peter I in 1698. The chains and stars from that order are displayed on the door, and there some St. Andrew crosses on top of the columns. This is the throne room — the heart of the Kremlin. On coronation days, this was where the emperor and first lady received greetings from their subjects. The emperor's armchair, carved in the traditional Russian style, stood here until the end of the 19th century, when it was replaced by three chairs under a canopy with ermine curtains, one each for Emperor Nicholas II, Empress Alexandra, and widowed Empress Maria, the emperor's mother. Their personal monograms were carved into the backrests. The back of the curtains displayed a double eagle. Above the canopy, the national

Modern look of St. Andrew Hall after restoration (left) and the Convention Room of the Supreme Soviet of the USSR and RSFSR, created in the 1930s by merging St. Alexander and St. Andrew Halls. The imperial thrones were replaced by a 10-meter statue of Lenin

Inside St. Catherine Hall

emblem of Russia was displayed with arch-angels on either side, the inscription "God with us," and emblems of all the lands and kingdoms of Russia. Above all this, there was the image of the "all-seeing eye" in a halo — the Orthodox symbol of the Holy Trinity. One of the palace grenadiers on duty was to remain by the throne at all times. All those fortunate enough to be admitted to the palace today will be able to see all of this, except the grenadier. Incidentally, the Order of St. Andrew the First Called was reinstated as Russia's supreme award in 1998, and St. Andrew Hall resumed its ceremonial duties a little later, when President Vladimir Putin had his inauguration here.

The wraparound gallery contiguous to the St. Alexander and St. Andrew Halls was dismantled in the 1930s, when the rooms were merged. At the end of the 1990s, the gallery and the service building in the inner yard were remodeled once again according to a design concept created by artist Ilya Glazunov, who fashioned several smaller official rooms in the service building, called Petrovsky, Shtofny, Kaminny, Red and Green, intended for miscellaneous receptions and talks. The lobby became a gallery again — this time somewhat more pompous looking than during the imperial era. The walls are now adorned by portraits of Russian rulers for the last ten centuries, from Prince Rurik to Nicholas II, all painted by Ilya Glazunov's son Ivan.

Heading north out of St. Andrew Hall, we find ourselves in the Cavalry Guard Hall. This was where military guards stayed when the emperor was in the palace. The emperor's personal guards were traditionally recruited from among Cherkes nationals — a proud mountain folk from the Caucasus, which explains why the original furniture in the Cavalry Guard Hall, including the sofa and the chairs, was made from plane wood from the Caucasus. The painting on the wall showed Czar Alexius inspecting his troops on parade by the Novodevichyi Convent in the 17th century. In the 1930s, the room was reappointed to hold NKVD secret police guards during official conventions and other events. The current furniture in this room is made from Karelian birch wood.

The empress's escort consisted of cavalry guards — tall, handsome officers in white uniforms, who guarded the part of the palace with St. Catherine Throne Hall and the empress's chambers. The empress's throne stood in St. Catherine Hall under a canopy of crimson velvet. (Its space by the easterly wall is currently vacant). The amazing antique standard lamps are still here. The room was dedicated to the Order of St. Catherine, founded by Peter I in 1714 in honor of his wife Catherine I. It is a known historical fact that in 1711, when Peter's Prut campaign ran into trouble, the would-be empress helped him save the Russian army from massive imprisonment by bribing the Turkish

The wraparound gallery was remodeled once again

Inside St. Vladimir Hall

commander with her jewelry. The Order of St. Catherine was only awarded to ladies. The rule was that no more than 12 persons could hold the Order of St. Catherine 1st Degree at the same time, apart from persons of royal blood. It was the honorary duty of St. Catherine chevalier ladies to be present at all gala ceremonies in this hall alongside ladies of the court. This hall looks familiar to us,

and no surprise: this is the venue of summit talks, and it's on TV quite frequently.

The suite down the hall is all decked out in gold on green and red with gold-plated furnishings: the main drawing room and the empress's bedroom. At the end of the suite, we pass through the official coat check, faced with tawny walnut panels, and enter the Freulein Corridor of the Terem Palace. The windows of the former maids' rooms face the corridor. In 1959, a Winter Garden of marble and mirrors with a fountain pond and over 120 tropical plants was fashioned at the end of the corridor. From here, a small staircase leads to the last official hall, named after the Order of the Holy Prince Vladimir, founded by Catherine II in 1782.

Due to its faintly rounded corners, this square hall seems octagonal. Its architecture welds three epochs, mirroring the buildings adjacent to it: the Terem Palace (16th–17th centuries), Granovitaya and Czarina's Gold Chambers (15th–16th centuries), and the Grand Kremlin Palace (19th century). This small hall, sized 16x16 m, occupies a part of what previously was Postelnoe Porch (also called Boyar Landing) — the place where the Boyars waited for the Czar. We also know St. Vladimir Hall from TV. Until recently, this was the place where various international treaties were signed. Before 1917, this was where the emperor ended his round of the palace and met with merchant and citizen envoys and petitioners.

The Red Drawing Room in the Empress's official chambers

О&БРАЗ ВЕЛИКАГО
ГДРА ЦРА ИВЕЛИКАГО
КНZА · АЛЕZ&А МIХАИЛОВI&
ВСЕА ВЕЛIКIА IМАЛ&А
IБ&Л&А РОСII САМОД&РЦА

Terem Palace

You can feel the air of ancient times emanating from the Terem Palace, standing behind the Granovitaya Chamber. This was the residence of Russian rulers up until the reign of Peter the Great. The palace cannot be seen from Cathedral Square. The best view of the Terem is from its inner courtyard or Ivan the Great Bell Tower, but none are open to the public. The Terem Palace itself is also unavailable, so we'll try to partially make up for the lack of first-hand experience with this profile of the Terem's history and interior.

History

The three-story Terem (or "Tower Chamber") Palace was built in 1635-1636 on top of an existing two-level structure dating back to the reigns of Vasily III and Ivan IV the Terrible (16th century). The bottom floors have since been remodeled so many times they have lost much of their original look. Czarevich Alexius Romanov was the first to move into the stone building, while his father Mikhail continued to live in the wooden part: he believed it was better for his health.

The new stone chambers were finished in 1637 with the walls painted on a gold and silver primer, and with multicolored mica windows crafted by the artist Ivan Osipov. Architects define the look of the Terem Palace as a motley blend of old Russian and Italian architecture (called "Lombardian" in medieval Russia).

The Terem Palace was erected inside the Royal Court, a sprawling estate with numerous buildings: churches, mansions, government offices, workshops and support services. The majority of the buildings were wooden, and almost each member of the Royal Family had their own artfully decorated house or terem. The Terem Palace was home to the Czar and his sons. The chambers inhabited by the Czarina and princesses, annexed to the northern side of the building, no longer exist. Back then, the front of the royal buildings faced Cathedral Square in the east, not the Moskva River in the south as it does now.

The Royal Court and Terem Palace thrived in the second half of the 17th century. According to overseas travelers, the roofs of all the Terems were gold-plated at the time. The buildings along Borovitsky Hill were topped with greenhouses and gardens redolent of the Gardens of Semiramis, the Queen of Babylon.

In the 18th century, the Terem Palace and the rest of the old royal estate gradually fell into decay. In 1737, during the reign of Anna, Ivan the Terrible's daughter, a devastating fire destroyed nearly all the buildings and severely damaged the Terems. Empress Elizabeth, Peter the Great's daughter, ordered the Italian architect Rastrelli to build a new royal palace where the Grand Kremlin Palace now stands. The Terems were repaired, and court servants with their families moved in.

Napoleon stayed in Elizabeth's Palace during the French invasion in 1812; then the French burned it down together with other buildings as they retreated from Moscow. The architect Konstantin Ton built the existing Grand Kremlin Palace to the order of Emperor Nicholas I in 1838-1849, joining it with the Terems. By their 200th anniversary, the Terems were remodeled and redecorated according to the original models and drawings from the reign of Alexius Romanov. A little later, in the 1870s, the artist Timofei Kiselev painted the existing murals on gold, deriving from drawings by Feodor Solntsev.

This look the Terem Palace and its churches had in the 19th century

◀— **The portrait of Czar Alexius**

Terem Palace

Inside the Terems

The Terem Palace is five stories tall. As in the Middle Ages, the two bottom floors are occupied by Kremlin household services. The third floor, which had housed the Czar's banya (bathroom) and his children's rooms in the 17th century and served as an official archive before the 1917 Revolution, is now devoted to logistics as well. The fourth floor has been redecorated to recreate the original royal chambers: the Hall (or Refectory), the Cross Room (or Duma Room), the Czar's office and bedroom. The fifth floor houses a structure known as "Golden Topped Teremok" with a wraparound open gallery, built by Czar Mikhail for his sons.

The whole building is permeated by the aura of an old wooden dwelling. It looks like several peasant huts one on top of the other. In the living quarters, almost all the rooms are alike, each having three windows like a typical hut. Only the Golden Topped Teremok on the top floor is one large, sun-filled room.

Before the end of the 17th century, the only people allowed to enter the living quarters on the 4th floor were the Czar and

The famous Gold lattice

his family members. The stairs first lead to the Verkhospassky landing with its famous Gold lattice. Few Russians have ever seen the fence up close, which, rumor had it, had been cast from devalued copper coins withdrawn from circulation by Czar Alexius in 1662 to stop the Copper Riots. (This was the Czar's idea of fighting inflation). But in fact, the lattice is gold-plated wrought iron, very artfully made. From a few meters away, it seems to be decorated with a purely floral ornament, but a closer inspection reveals strange fishes, birds and monsters.

Behind the lattice there is a porch with lion sculptures holding shields with the monogram of Nicholas I, whose reign saw the building remodeled so that the outdoor porch became "internalized." The Golden Porch had previously adjoined the goldsmith's workshop where various church accessories were made. A weight, shaped as a lion head with an apple in its mouth (symbolizing faithful keeping of royal secrets), is hanging from the vaulted ceiling over the porch stairs.

The Front Room with low vaulted ceilings and tiled furnaces is painted with images of the Byzantine Emperor Constantine and his mother Helen, the Russian Prince Vladimir and Princess Olga. This was the waiting room where Boyars waited for the Czar to follow him to the Cross Room, where they would take pews according to their rank.

Layout of the Terem Palace

1. Cellar
2. Utilities
3. Golden Porch
4. Golden Topped Teremok

The Cross Room was where the Czar received his blessing from a priest in the morning, and discussed affairs of the state, sitting on the throne, in the afternoon. Sometimes the Czar would receive foreign ambassadors here, but only those representing Christian nations.

The next room, called Golden Room in the 17th century, would most likely be called an office

The Petitioners' Window

today, but they don't make offices like this anymore. Its door used to be upholstered in gold-plated leather with images of plants and animals. In the left-hand corner next to the window stood the royal throne. The carpet in front of it was woven by the Czar's daughters. This was the room where more delicate issues were discussed, and where the Czar would treat the more loyal Boyars and feed beggars and "resident" pilgrims. Those pilgrims lived next to the royal residence, fully provided by the Czar. Leading a virtuous life, they sometimes lived to be 100 or older.

Another interesting detail about the Golden Room is its middle window, the one nearest to the throne, overlooking the inner courtyard and what was called Boyar Landing. On the outside, the window stands out with its carved white-stone window case with a double eagle. This was Petitioners' Window, from where a small box would be lowered down on a thread, where petitions could be dropped to go directly to the Czar.

The fourth room is the bedroom. Medallions on the walls display scenes of the Nativity of John the Precursor and Jesus Christ, St. Nicholas the Miracle-Worker as an infant, and other saints. The Czar slept on a rather small carved wooden bed behind a Chinese silk curtain at the head of the bed, bearing the words of King David from Psalm 44 in Greek. A young sword bearer would sing the psalm for King Saul to cheer him up. A small, winding staircase leads down to the Czar's banya, or bathroom, right underneath the bedroom. The floors and walls in the bathroom were waterproofed with lead slabs.

A side door leads to the praying room. The window frames of the two adjacent rooms are still glazed with mica, or "Russian glass." According to anecdotal evidence, this used to be the pantry for food and beverages, including Malmsey and Rheinwein, the favorite wines of Czar Mikhail and his son Alexius which they were happy to share with their boyar visitors.

The Golden Topped Teremok on the top (5th) floor is one large room — a kind of a penthouse standing on the flat roof of the Terem Palace, surrounded by a gallery. A Watchtower with multicolored stained glass windows adjoins it from the west. The carved decorations, which doubled as amusements for the Czar's children, depict fabled, mythical creatures: centaurs with bows and arrows, satyrs with tails and hooves, parrots in grapevine thickets, and so on.

Interior of the Cross Room

Terem Palace

The Life of Russian Czars at the Kremlin

In the 17th century, influences of Byzantium could be felt in every part of the Terem Palace. There was a rigorous order and hierarchy in everything. Any breach of the etiquette, even just a foul word spoken here could have been construed as an insult to the Czar, and a cause for disfavor. There were secret eavesdropping contraptions everywhere to prevent conspiracy and intrigue.

    The day of a Czar of Muscovy was quite traditional. The Czar woke up at dawn with the first rays of the sun — at 4 or 5 in the morning in summer, and no later than 7 in winter. The candles were already on by the icons in the Cross Room. On the lectern lay the icon of the event or saint whose memorial day it was. The Czar would pray for about 15 minutes, then receive the priest's blessing that came with a sprinkle of holy water, specially delivered from some remote monastery or sacred place. Then the Czar, sometimes with the Czarina, would proceed to one of the court churches for the morning prayer or early mass. On major holidays, the Czar would go to one of the Kremlin churches instead. A mass lasted two hours. During the Lent or other fasting periods, Alexius Romanov would stay in church five hours in a row, giving as many as a thousand bows. There was no breakfast as

Tiled stove of the Golden Room

such, because no eating was allowed before church, and the service took so long it was already near lunchtime when it was over. After church, the Czar attended to his daily business until around noon. Sometimes he would receive foreign ambassadors. Representatives of Christian nations would enter via the Annunciation Church, which was linked to the royal palace. Non-Christians used a different staircase that then existed

Czar Mikhail confers with Boyars in the Terem Palace

between the Annunciation Church and the Granovitaya Chamber.

When he was done with business, the Czar proceeded to the refectory. On fasting days, the food consisted of oatmeal mash with rye bread; the beverages were wine, beer or apple juice. On regular days, as many as 70 dishes would be served, including caviar, chowder, charbroiled meat, and so on. During major fasting periods (four times a year), even lean, scanty meals were served only three times a week; the rest of the week, food was limited to pickled mushrooms with half a glass of beer. After the meal, the Czar would retire for a nap, usually until around 3:00 pm, in line with the Oriental custom. Unlike Russia, noon is the hottest time of the day in the East. After the nap, the Czar's servants returned and they went to vespers together. Then he would attend to government affairs again for a couple of hours. Later in the evening, the Czar spent time with his family, read religious books, or listened to pilgrims' stories about their pilgrimages in far-off lands, sphinxes and "people with dog heads" they had seen somewhere in Egypt. Sometimes he would play chess or see a circus show. After the eve-

Golden bowl was a gift of Czar Alexius to Patriarch Nikon in 1653

ning meal, the Czar proceeded to the Cross Chamber, where he had started his day, for his evening prayer.

The Czarina and princesses also followed the traditional daily routine. In fact, they were rarely allowed to leave the palace at all; there were rigorous restrictions they had to follow even inside the royal estate. No courtier, except the Czar, could talk to them directly. All communication was through a boyar confidante. One of the few joys for the Czarina and princesses were gala processions to church, where they could parade their best dresses, albeit to no audience as the Kremlin would be completely sealed off on those occasions. This went on century after century, until Peter the Great came and ended this lifestyle forever. In Russia's new capital - St. Petersburg - court life would be completely different, more European.

Czarina's Golden Chamber

The Czarina's reception room, or Golden Chamber, adjoining the Terem Palace from the east, was first mentioned in the chronicles in 1526, when it was called Naugolnaya (Corner) Chamber. The chamber was rebuilt

Interior of Czarina's Golden Chamber

for Czarina Irina Godunova, Czar Feodor's wife and Boris Godunov's sister, in the 1580s, when the murals on gold were also painted, which gave the room its name. As we enter we immediately travel four hundred years or so back in time. Low vaulted ceilings, gilded murals, narrow windows, and twilight... It feels like only days ago, the Czarina, the Czar, the Patriarch and courtiers exchanged triple kisses here at Easter, in accordance with the Russian tradition. As many as a hundred or more people would approach the Czarina for a triple kiss, one by one. That's why her chamber was built so roomy. On

Eleven gilded cupolas of the court churches and three windows of the Czarina's Golden Chamber overlook the Cathedral Square between the Faceted Chamber and the Church of Deposition of the Robe

the walls and ceilings: sacred images and stylized portraits of Byzantine Empresses Irina, Theodora and Sophia; Georgian Queen Dinara; Russian Princess Olga, the first Rurik descendant to have received Baptism in Constantinople in 955; scenes from the history of Christianity featuring Byzantine Emperor Constantine and his mother Helen.

Russian Czarinas received their esteemed guests, hosted wedding ceremonies and holiday receptions here. When a Czarina passed away, her wake would also be held here.

In 1683, the ceilings in the Golden Chamber were reinforced with solid crisscrossed arches and iron supports, running quite low. This destroyed the harmony of the room, but had to be done when the chamber was built up with some churches.

Court Churches

(None of the churches at the Terem Palace hold services anymore, except the Church of the Deposition of the Robe in Cathedral Square)

The eleven gilded domes you can see from Palace Square right of the Granovitaya Chamber form three contiguous sets of five domes each, crowning a number of small churches that used to be the in-house temples for the Czars and their family members.

St. Catherine's Church is on the first floor, with the Church of the Resurrection di-

rectly above it. These two churches are assigned the five right-hand (northern) domes of 11. The Church of Our Savior Behind the Golden Trellis, or Verkhospassky Cathedral, is on the second level. It has a John the Precursor altar, arranged above Czarina's Gold Chamber. This church owns the five left-hand (southern) domes. The Church of the Crucifixion (Raising of the Cross) has the central dome, which also forms a set of five with the four domes around it, belonging to the other churches.

Church of Our Savior Behind the Gold Lattice (Verkhospassky Cathedral)

This used to be a standalone church with entrance from the Boyar Landing in the west, which is now inside the palace buildings. The name of the church came from the

Iconostasis of the Vekhospassky Cathedral

famous Gold lattice, separating it from the landing. Its other name — Verkhospassky (Upper Savior's) Cathedral — means that the church is located on the third floor of the Terem Palace.

The Church of Our Savior Not Made by Hand was built concurrently with the Terem Palace during the reign of Czar Mikhail Romanov in 1635–1636, to be used as his house church. Russian rulers from Mikhail to Peter the Great visited this church quite frequently.

Its luxurious carved, gold-plated iconostasis was crafted by Dmitry Shiryaev in the 18th century. It is one of the few Kremlin iconostases having survived the 1812 rampage and subsequent fires and destruction.

The church was renovated and remodeled several times. Nicholas I ordered its interior repainted in 1836. Only the northern and southern walls still contain fragments of 1670 murals.

Before the 1917 Revolution, the Church of Our Savior was open for public prayer only once a year, on its church holiday.

The altar cross (1667) was a gift of Czar Feodor to Verkhospassky Cathedral

St. Catherine's Church

When the wooden church that had stood here before burned down again, Czar Mikhail in 1627 ordered a more solid church built here in honor of the celestial patron of his wife, Czarina Eudokia.

The church, standing on the northern side of the Czarina's Gold Chamber, was designed by English architect John Tyler.

The church was re-consecrated in the name of St. Catherine during the reign of Alexius, when it became the house church for Czarinas and princesses. This was where female members of the royal family came for what was called "purifying prayers" after childbirth and when fasting.

The existing church interior was created in the 1840s, when Nicholas I was Czar, while construction was in progress on the Grand Kremlin Palace. The colored glass inserts in the iconostasis are an imitation of gems. Of all the accoutrements of this church, only the precious crown from the Icon of St. Catherine, strewn with emeralds, diamonds and sapphires, is on public display, being located at the publicly accessible Armory.

Church of the Resurrection

In 1681, Czar Feodor, the son of Alexius, ordered St. Eudokia's altar above St. Catherine's Church re-consecrated in honor of an important religious highlight, Rejuvenation of the Church of the Resurrection in Jerusalem (this holiday is also called Resurrection Day). The new church was part of the Czar's bigger plan to recreate the main sanctuaries of Jerusalem on the Terem estate. Following up on the same idea, a semblance of the Golgotha was fashioned in between the Resurrection Church and Verkhospassky Cathedral with a carved cypress Crucifix. The Golgotha replica rested on an alabaster base, painted to look like marble. In front of the Crucifix, the Shroud was placed on the pillars. Sixty cherubs with golden wings were hanged on wires above. The air from the flames of twelve oil lamps made the cherubs go slowly round, their wings aglitter. The paintings along the wall depicted scenes from the Gospel: Descent into Hell, the Resurrection, Assumption and Christ

Iconostasis of the St. Catherine Church

Carved iconostasis of the Church of the Resurrection and the Holy Doors

Appearing before Virgin Mary. The entire composition was dismantled later.

The key landmark in the church is its unique 17th century iconostasis, the work of a team of carvers led by Klim Mikhailov. It is a piece of tremendous beauty, unmatched at the Kremlin. The intricate carving was plated with gold and silver and painted so artfully it looks like porcelain or mother of pearl. Next to it is an old silver church chandelier — a gift to Czar Alexius from Karl XI, the King of Sweden.

Church of the Crucifixion (Raising of the Cross)

This tiny church, sized only 25 square meters, adjoins the Church of the Resurrection above the Verkhospassky Cathedral. The icon on canvas inside the altar is The Adoration of the Cross. The images on the icon are those of the Byzantine Emperor St. Constantine and his mother, St. Helen. Next to them are Czar Alexius, his first wife Maria, and Patriarch Nikon.

The carved golden iconostasis contains

Icon of the Adoration of the Cross

unique 17th century icons. Only the faces and hands of the saints were painted; their vestments and the background were made from silk fabric of varying texture with inserts of beads and small pearls. Historians assume that the icon painter, Vasily Poznansky, may have modeled his icons on certain Flemish engravings, and had possibly learned the appliqué technique from the Russian Czarinas or nuns at the Ascension Convent.

Flanking the iconostasis, two unusual icons rest inside their dedicated frames, depicting Virgin Mary allegorically as the Moon, and Christ, as the Sun. The Moon and the Son are shown at their feet. While the majority of images depict the passions of Christ on the Golgotha, the general décor creates a peaceful, light hearted ambience in this church.

Church of the Nativity of Our Lady

This old church tucked away in the remotest, western part of the Terem Palace is crowned with a golden

Interior the Church of the Nativity of Our Lady

remodeling projects in the 19th century.

Count Leo Tolstoy and Sofia Bers, the daughter of Emperor Alexander II's private doctor, had their wedding ceremony here in 1862.

Church of the Resurrection of Lazarus

This 14th century temple, the oldest church on Kremlin grounds, is located on the bottom floor, underneath the Church of the Nativity of Virgin Mary. Before the Ascension Convent was built, this church had served as the burial vault for female members of the ruling family. The treasury was also stored here. In the 17th century the church was closed, and remained forgotten for over 200 years. When the bottom floor of the Terems was explored in 1842 for the building of a new Kremlin Palace, the builders found the ancient vaults and altar of the forgotten church. Emperor Nicholas I ordered the church rebuilt in its original shape, and consecrated for the Resurrection of Lazarus. From then on, the church ranked among the palace churches, holding services once a year, on Lazarus Saturday.

dome. It was built in stone in 1393–1394 to the order of Princess Eudokia, the wife of Prince Dmitry Donskoy, to replace an earlier St. Lazarus wooden church.

The church, which had burned many times, acquired its present look in 1681-1684, when the original structure by Aloysius was replaced with a new top temple, built by Feodor Tikhonov. Weak light percolates from the outside through the dome and the barred windows with a medieval ornament. The lower row of windows, overlooking the palace hallway, are glazed with multicolored glass. The walls and vaulted ceilings are covered with ornaments and images of the saints. The church's silver iconostasis was made by the architect Konstantin Ton to the order of Nicholas I. The icons were painted in the late 19th century academic style, while the stucco moldings and the two tiled furnaces are older and more traditional. The Holy Doors is one of the few genuinely old artifacts having survived multiple

The Church of the Deposition of the Robe (15th century)

Church of the Deposition of the Robe

(The only church open to general public; services are held once a year, on its church day, July 15)
This small church with one dome, standing across from the western entrance to the Assumption Cathedral, is linked to the Grand Kremlin and Terem Palaces. An inner vestibule ("Patriarch's Passageways") was built into its northern side. The Czars

Among the sacred carved objects the icon of Crucifixion (18th century) from the demolished Chudov (Miracle) Monastery is now on display in the Church of the Deposition of the Robe

Kiev and Vladimir to Moscow. The other pillar depicts the eight Russian Metropolitans canonized as saints. Above all the Russian saints are images of the saints who were namesakes of Romanov family members.

The four-level iconostasis no longer has its original frame, but has retained most of its icons, created in 1627 by a group of icon painters supervised by Nazarius Istomin to the order of Patriarch Philaret. The 16th century Holy Doors adorning the iconostasis of the Church of the Deposition of the Robe today, was transferred here from the Church of Our Savior on the Bor, destroyed in the 1930s.

Above its "resident" icons, the iconostasis currently hosts a large selection of 16th–18th century miniature icons.

and Patriarchs used the vestibule to go to the Assumption Cathedral for prayer. Later on, when St. Petersburg became the new capital, visiting Emperors and Empresses would also use it for the same purpose.

This church used to be the house temple of the Metropolitans of Moscow and Russia and then, from 1589 on, of the Russian Orthodox Patriarchs. The church owed its dedication to the Holiday of the Deposition of the Robe of Our Lady to an important event in Russian history. In July 1451, troops led by the Tartar Prince Mazovshi approached Moscow, but then suddenly retreated.

The look of this church is typical for small, single-dome churches built in the 15th–16th centuries. The 1644 murals have survived almost intact, depicting scenes from the earthly life of Virgin Mary, glorifying her miraculous powers. One of the pillars features the images of Russian princes canonized as saints. The images in the bottom row are of the first Russian saints, the princes and martyrs Boris and Gleb, whom their brother Sviatopolk had ordered killed. Then come George, the Prince of Vladimir, who was killed in a battle with the Tartars; and Czarevich Dmitry, who died in Uglich. The images express the idea of martyrdom for Christ and for your faith. In the top row Russian saint princes are depicted: Vladimir the Baptiser of Rus, Andrei Bogoliubsky, Alexander Nevsky and Daniil Aleksandrovich, illustrating succession of power from

Interior of the Church of the Deposition of the Robe. The copper church-chandelier with double eagle was made in 1624 to the order of Patriarch Philaret

Granovitaya (Faceted) Chamber

Standing between the Churches of the Assumption and the Annunciation, the Granovitaya Chamber's westerly wall is contiguous to the Grand Kremlin Palace. From the reign of Grand Prince Ivan III on, it served as the official throne room. The chamber is now closed to general public.

Built with a high basement, Granovitaya Chamber was designed in 1487–1491 by the Italian architects Marco Ruffo and Pietro Solari. The name Granovitaya, or faceted, comes from the white stones in its façade, which were cut to a rectangular shape in the style of Italian Renaissance architecture. This technique is also known as "diamond-shape rustication." The chamber was also called Our Lord's Gold Chamber as its vaulted ceilings were painted gold in the 17th century.

Many centuries ago, the Granovitaya Chamber was the seat of the Boyar Duma; it also hosted Land Assemblies, official receptions and celebrations in honor of victorious military leaders. Following the coronation, Russian rulers and their spouses would throw a royal dinner at the Granovitaya Chamber for the nobility and commoners alike.

Red Porch

The beautiful 'Red' Porch would be covered with a red carpet for coronations. After the coronation ceremony at the Cathedral of the Assumption, the monarch would climb to the porch and bow down low to the people, crowding Cathedral Square. The Red Porch entrance was closed on regular days, and is permanently closed now.

There are two double eagles above the side pediments of the porch. In the bays of the stone hand-rails stand stone lions, once again evoking medieval Italian architecture. The golden Red Stairs with 43 steps and 3 landings lead up to the "Sacred Anteroom," where an image of St. George on horseback is carved above the entrance.

Sacred Anteroom

The Anteroom is an elongated room where the strongman received his visitors. This is where Kremlin priests blessed the monarchs after coronation and before important public appearances. The Sacred Anteroom was so named because its walls were covered with murals on biblical subjects. The old frescoes did not survive, so in 1847, the artist Feodor Zavialov repainted the walls. Three murals

There used to be a gold-plated wood awning above the Red Porch, which is the main entrance to the Granovitaya Chamber, but it burned down in the 1737 Trinity fire and was never restored

repeated the original motifs — the Old Testament Trinity, Archangel Michael Appearing before Jesus, and Constantine's Dream — thanks to an inventory drawn up by Simon Ushakov, the court icon artist, in the 17th century. Another two murals commemorated two events from Russian history: Sergius of Radonezh Blessing Dmitry Donskoy for the Battle of Kulikovo and Kiev Prince Vladimir Choosing his Faith.

There is a tiny secret room above the Anteroom, from where Tsarinas and Princesses could secretly watch through a barred window as the ruler received overseas ambassadors, and also when events were held that did not allow for their presence.

The Russian for 'Sacred Anteroom is 'Sviatye seni,' deriving from the Slavic word 'sen' that means 'roof' or 'cover'

The six carved gold-plated door portals add to the luxury and majesty of the Sacred Anteroom, but three of the portal are faux, made for the sake of symmetry in the 19th century. The real doors lead to the Granovitaya Chamber, St. Vladimir Hall of the Grand Kremlin Palace, and the Terem Palace.

Inside the Chamber

The whole chamber is a sprawling rectangular hall sized 495 square meters, spanned by four cruciform vaults, resting on a central pillar. All the walls and ceilings of this majestic hall are covered in murals. The magnificent frescoes on various subjects from the history of Russia and Christianity cannot fail to impress anyone who is fortunate enough to see them. The frescoes, painted by the Belousov brothers, specially invited by Alexander III from Palekh, Vladimir Region, also repeated the original frescoes according to Ushakov's inventory.

From the westerly vault, Lord Sabaoth is looking down, surrounded by a hierarchy of nine celestial ranks: Angels, Archangels, Cherubs, Seraphs, Dominations, Powers, Domains, Altars and Thrones. Some other frescoes are devoted to the Creation. As the vault inclines, motifs change from celestial to mortal, showing the Forefathers, the Prophets and the Evangelists. Then come scenes from Russian history and the Bible.

The frescoes on the easterly side illustrate The Tale of the Princes of Vladimir, a 16th century epic propagating the sacerdotal nature of the Kingdom of Muscovy, the "Third Rome" and heir to Rome and Constantinople, the ancient strongholds of Christianity. On the walls, we see the earliest Ruriks, who ruled Russia in the 9th through 10th centuries: the original Rurik himself, then Igor, Sviatoslav and Vladimir, who converted Russia to Christianity in 988, bringing it spiritually closer to the rest of Europe.

Another scene from The Tale on the southerly wall shows the bringing of royal symbols of power from Byzantium to Russia, symbolizing the succession of power between Byzantine Emperors and Moscow rulers. On the southeastern part of the wall, there is a painting of Feodor, the son of Ivan the Terrible, who was the last of the Rurik family. Next to him is Boris Godunov, the Czarina's

View of the Chamber and entrance to the Sacred Anteroom

brother, who ruled Russia in tandem with Feodor.

Historians believe the Old Testament scene with Joseph the Beautiful on the northern side of the chamber also has something to do with Boris Godunov. Joseph was as wise as he was beautiful. He became an advisor to the Egyptian Pharaoh, and later received a royal coronet from his hands. The scene shows how a wise man can become Czar even if he is not of royal blood. It is a known fact that Boris Godunov started as a royal stableman, and eventually became Czar.

The frescoes on the westerly wall illustrate the parables about the just and unjust judges. One virtuous judge urged the ruler to be fair, and the ruler punished a relative of his for not having appeared in court to answer to a plea from a common woman. A sinful judge took a bribe — a precious goblet and a sack of silver — and sent an innocent person to prison. The judge is having a feast, while his soul is on its way to hell. The scene reminds everyone that on Judgment Day, every man will have to answer for his deeds, no matter how high he may have been in the earthly hierarchy.

The artwork on the window jambs shows 24 exponents of the Rurik family, among them: Prince Daniel (Alexander Nevsky's son), Ivan Kalita, Dmitry Donskoy, Ivan III and Ivan the Terrible, Russia's glorious rulers.

The central pillar is decorated with painted, gold-plated white stone bas reliefs. Creatures from the three elements — earth, water and the sky — represent the merits of a worthy ruler. The dolphin is the symbol of a ruler who takes good care of his subjects. The deer symbolizes power and authority; the crane means wisdom and prudence; the pelican stands for selfless love; and the winged half-snake, half-lion symbolizes the union of wisdom and power.

Originally the pillar was surrounded by racks of shelves filled with gold and silver goblets, plates and other tableware. In early Russia, tableware was second only to icons in importance in any dwelling. The hosts loved to show off their rich tableware to impress their guests.

The room has 18 windows, 4 old vintage dark-bronze church chandeliers and 20 candleholders on the walls.

Ivan the Terrible, Catherine the Great and other Russian rulers threw lavish feasts here. The last royal party was held here to celebrate the coronation of Emperor Nicholas II on 14 May 1896.

The Granovitaya Chamber is still used in accordance with its original intent. The President of Russia hosts dinners here in honor of visiting foreign heads of state.

Granovitaya Chamber

A royal dinner at the Granovitaya Chamber. 1856

Patriarch's Palace and Twelve Apostles' Church

The shortcut from the Troitskie (Trinity) Gate to Cathedral Square lies under the vaults of the Patriarshie (Patriarch's) Gate in the Twelve Apostles' Church, which is part of the Patriarch's Palace, housing museum exhibits representing the everyday life of affluent Muscovites in the 17th century. Some of the exhibits belonged to eminent historic figures.

History

From the 14th century on, before the Patriarch's Palace was built, this was the estate of Peter, the first Metropolitan of Russia, replaced in 1448 by the stone chambers of His Eminence Metropolitan Jonah, who stood at the helm of the Russian Orthodox Church after it became independent from the Constantinople Patriarchs. After the institution of Patriarchy was introduced in Russia in 1589, during the reign of Feodor, the estate came to be known as the Patriarch's Chambers.

The existing Patriarch's Palace was erected in 1655, when Nikon was Patriarch, replacing the old, more modest building. (Nikon thought his predecessors' abode did not do justice to his high stature as a statesman). The magnificent stone building rose higher than all Boyar houses in the Kremlin. In size and luxury, the Patriarch's Palace was only matched by the royal Terem Palace. Inside the Patriarch's Palace, the Cross Chamber was the most luxuriously decorated room. Unfortunately for Nikon, he only lived amid this luxury for two

The Church of the Twelve Apostles at the Patriarch's Palace. An Icon of Our Savior Not-Made-by-Hand was originally painted on the wall above the gate

years. Having fallen out with Czar Alexius in 1658, Nikon resigned as Patriarch and left Moscow for good.

The Patriarch's estate thrived under Nikon, numbering dozens of buildings, including bakeries, breweries, wineries, icon painting studios, homeless shelters, guesthouses for visiting foreigners and new converts, and even fruit orchards.

Half a century later, in 1721 (Patriarch Adrian died in 1700), Peter I abolished Patriarchy. The former Patriarch's Palace and estate was re-subordinated to the Holiest Synod, the body established to run the Russian Orthodox Church. The Moscow Synod Office moved in. The Palace would lose its original splendor over the years that followed.

In 1763, the luxurious Cross Chamber was reappointed as a workshop to produce myrrh, a special scented church oil, and renamed Myrrh Boiling Chamber.

In the 1950s, restoration artists whitewashed over the latest murals in the Twelve Apostles' Church, restoring the church's historic 17th century look. Only a few fragments of 17th century murals were left intact inside the central dome. The floor was paved with glazed tiles, modeled on 1681 vintage tiles found inside the altar. The vaults in the Myrrh Boiling Chamber were painted with floral ornaments.

The first level used to house various household services and the Patriarch's offices. The Grand Chamber on the first level, which you enter from the northerly façade, is now an exhibition venue.

A steep, narrow staircase leads to the upstairs hall, from where you can enter the

← **This portrait of Patriarch Nikon and his staff used to hang in the Patriarch's private chambers. One of the priests is holding a pair of glasses – then a brand new invention that had just appeared in Russia.**

Cross Chamber or the Twelve Apostles' Church across the hall. The entire second level, including the Myrrh Boiling Chamber, is a Museum of 17th Century Russian Applied Arts and Household Utensils.

Cross (Myrrh Boiling) Chamber

Nikon had his Cross Chamber modeled on Czar Alexius' Granovitaya Chamber, but unlike the latter, it was built with a single vaulted ceiling sized around 280 square meters, converging in the middle but with no supporting pillar. An iconostasis was built adjoining the easterly wall with a large cross standing next to it that gave the chamber its original name (this was the traditional way cross chambers were appointed in monasteries). The floor was covered with multicolored tiles; the windows were glazed with thin mica (also called "Russian glass"); and the window trellises were adorned with colorful satin flowers.

Land Assemblies were held at the Granovitaya Chamber, while the Cross

Patriarch Nikon's crown-shaped mitre — a gift from Czar Alexius

Chamber hosted Church (or Consecrated) Assemblies. The Czar threw his official receptions and lavish feasts at his Granovitaya Chamber, while the Patriarch used the Cross Chamber, which doubled as the Patriarch's main office on regular days.

The Cross Chamber boasts a plethora of exhibits, such as icon settings, church utensils, silverware, clocks, etc. Among the exhibits on display, one finds artifacts like a silver, gold-plated ladle that belonged to Czar Mikhail, or a frying pan of impressive dimensions, believed to have been used to make pancakes at Shrove-Tide. Next to all this, there is a collection of 16th–17th century Russian and foreign-made clocks and watches, including the clocks that belonged to Czars Ivan the Terrible and Alexius, and Patriarchs Philaret and Nikon.

One of the showcases contains Patriarch Nikon's white klobuk (headdress) with pearl-embroidered images of Jesus Christ, the Holy Virgin, and John the Precursor, along with the Patriarchs of Moscow and

View and layout of the Patriarch's Palace and Twelve Apostles' Church in the 17th and 18th centuries, before patriarchy was abolished

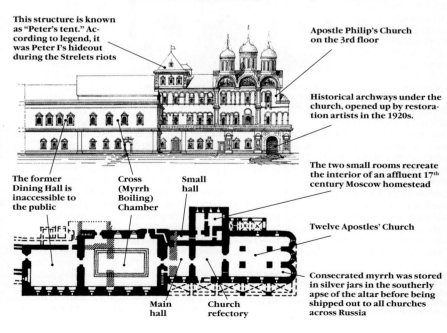

This structure is known as "Peter's tent." According to legend, it was Peter I's hideout during the Strelets riots

Apostle Philip's Church on the 3rd floor

Historical archways under the church, opened up by restoration artists in the 1920s.

The two small rooms recreate the interior of an affluent 17th century Moscow homestead

Twelve Apostles' Church

Consecrated myrrh was stored in silver jars in the southerly apse of the altar before being shipped out to all churches across Russia

The former Dining Hall is inaccessible to the public

Cross (Myrrh Boiling) Chamber

Small hall

Main hall

Church refectory

Contemporary view of the Cross (Myrrh Boiling) Chamber with a decorated silver tub — a gift from Empress Catherine II

the Universe. The earflaps on the klobuk symbolize a monk's aloofness to secular temptations. By the right-hand wall in the middle of the Cross (Myrrh Boiling) Chamber stands an 18th century myrrh making oven next to a massive silver tub with cast decorations — a gift from Empress Catherine II.

Once every three years, myrrh was prepared at the Cross Chamber for all Russian Orthodox churches. Myrrh was prepared with as many as 50 ingredients, including unction oil (olive oil), white wine, fragrant extracts of tropical tree bark, scented oils and balms, rose petals, Our Lady's Grass, and other herbs and fragrances.

From Great Monday through Great Wednesday on Passions Week, myrrh would be boiled in silver cauldrons while the Gospel was read non-stop. Then fragrances were added, and the myrrh was ladled into twelve silver kungan vessels for the Twelve Apostles. Consecrated myrrh was dispensed to all Russian Orthodox churches across Russia to be used as necessary.

Consecrated myrrh was used to anoint all Russian Czars for the throne in a special ritual. It was also used to consecrate churches. Myrrh is still prepared — largely according to the same method and recipe — once every three or four years at the Maly (Small) Cathedral of Moscow's Donskoi Monastery.

Twelve Apostles' Church

(divine services are held at the Twelve Apostles' Church once a year, on 13 July, Altar Day)

Leaving the Cross Chamber, we are back in the hall, from where we can walk on to the refectory of the Patriarch's house church. Patriarch Nikon had his majestic 5-dome Twelve Apostles' Church modeled on the Church of the Assumption (save that two of the domes are for decoration only, serving no functional purpose). But Nikon did not rule to see the church completely finished, which was done under Patriarch Joachim, who consecrated the church in the name of the Twelve Apostles in 1680.

The refectory currently houses a display of 17th century decorative ornamental embroidery, as well as church utensils such as patens (trays for consecrated bread), chalices (bowls for communion wine), large church fans with images of six-winged cherubs (symbolizing the presence of divine forces at consecration of the Holy Gifts), and others.

Decorative, or "personalized" embroidery involved two stages. Images were created by one group of artists, called "znamenshchiks," while ornaments were etched by "travshchik" artists. This kind of embroidery was usually made with expensive imported gold (gilded silver) threads and silk for affluent families — those of princes and boyars. Boyar wives and even Czarinas were themselves skilled embroiderers.

More mundane, purely ornamental embroidery used plainer supplies, such as canvas or flax threads, and was a common craft practiced in many Russian homes.

In 1929 the iconostasis of the Church of the Twelve Apostles was replaced by the one from the cathedral of the demolished Ascension monastery

Patriarch's Palace

Icon of the Crucifixion with Passions of the Apostles, relocated from the Church of the Assumption. Feodor Nikitin Rozhnov, 1699

The gold-plated iconostasis of the Twelve Apostles Church with an artfully carved grapevine was transferred here from the Church of the Ascension in the eponymous convent at the Kremlin, demolished in 1929. This explains why there is an 18th century icon of the Ascension where the Twelve Apostles' church icon should be.

The church walls are decked with more than twenty 17th century icons that are not historically related to the church. The icons, painted by Simon Ushakov, Kirill Ulanov, Feodor Zubov and other court icon painters, were collected from various churches.

17th century home interiors

The two small rooms adjacent to the refectory recreate the interior of an affluent 17th

A room in an affluent Moscow homestead, 17th century

century Moscow homestead, featuring a variety of household implements and decorations. A typical 17th century rich homestead was furnished with tables, wooden benches along the walls, and chests (usually for valuables and jewelry); it was filled with household utensils, clothing, books and official documents. Chairs, armchairs, cabinets, and other furniture from Western Europe first came to Russia in the mid-17th century. Later on, Russian carpenters would also learn to make this kind of furniture. The walls, doors and windows were upholstered with colored fabric to make the room look more cheerful, and the oven was finished with colored tiles. In the 17th century, it became customary to hang portraits on the walls as well as icons. The portrait in the first room is of the Czar's stolnik (court post) and envoy P.I. Potiomkin; the horseback portrait in the next room is of Czar Alexius.

Patriarch's rooms

The Patriarch's private chambers on the third level were heated by warm air rising through ducts from the ovens on the ground floor. This was the repository of many sacred manuscripts and relics. The chambers are not available for public tours. From the private chambers, a small passage leads to the former house temple of the Patriarchs — the Church of the Holy Apostle Philip.

Church of the Holy Apostle Philip

Consecrated by Patriarch Nikon in 1656 in the name of the Holy Apostle Philip, the house church is located on the third level of the Patriarch's Palace, directly above the refectory of the Twelve Apostles' Church. It is closed to general public. Apostle Philip was considered the celestial patron of St. Philip, the Metropolitan of

Byzantine icon of Apostle Philip (12th century)

Moscow, whom Nikon held in great esteem. Metropolitan Philip had publicly criticized Ivan the Terrible for the atrocities of his "oprichniki" brute squads that terrorized Russia, for which he was exiled to the Otroch Monastery near Tver. While in exile, Philip refused to bless Ivan the Terrible's war campaign against Novgorod and Pskov, and was eventually strangled by the Czar's hangman Maliuta Skuratov.

The precious late 16th — early 17th century chrismatory with myrrh that used to stand atop the altar is now on display in the Cross Chamber.

The life of Russian Orthodox Patriarchs at the Kremlin

A Russian Patriarch's daily routine was typical for all Russians at the time. The Patriarch woke up before dawn and went to church for the morning prayer. The Patriarch's working day began at around 6:00 am. There

was no breakfast as such. According to the Russian tradition, a priest can only officiate at a liturgy on an empty stomach, and Patriarchs had to officiate almost every day. The Patriarch received all sorts of visitors, irrespective of status and rank, until around 10:00 am. According to visitor logs, among the Patriarch's visitors

17th century jug

were metropolitans, archimandrites, rank-and-file priests, courtiers of title, Cossack atamans, esauls and regular Cossacks.

Petitioners seeking various jobs or appointments came first. The Patriarch would interview and test them on the spot. If he thought the applicant was right, the Patriarch would inscribe "worthy" on the petition. In some cases, the Patriarch would also divest people of rank or sack them on the spot for various misdemeanors.

Some petitioners sought the Patriarch's blessing for their marriage. Czar Alexius was one, asking the Patriarch to bless his proposed matrimony with Natalia Kirillovna. Ignatius Vasiliev, a clerk from the Nativity Church, was another.

The Patriarch also gave his blessing for public service, new construction and new home starts, and

frequently gave gifts of icons.

Many visitors brought the Patriarch their Name Day pies, baked on the morning of their Name Day specially for the Patriarch's appointment. It was customary to give every Name Day visitor an icon.

At 10:00 am, the Patriarch would administer a liturgy at his house church or any other church in town, wherever he was invited. On church holidays, liturgies were served at the Cathedral of the Assumption.

Patriarch Iov's panagia, a gift from Czar Feodor and Czarina Irina Godunova on the occasion of Iov's anointment for patriarchy. The panagia is a Byzantine cameo with the Crucifixion, painted on a double-layered agate (12th century) in a gold setting (16th century)

Noon was dinner time for the Patriarch. Most of the dishes were prepared with fish or mushrooms, with dough or dairy desserts.

On fasting days, 10 or so dishes would be served; on ferial days, as many as 30. Some of the favorite drinks were white

Rhine wine, sweet muscatel, beer brewed from barley with hops and mint, and various homemade fruit and honey beverages.

On holidays, tables for the guests were laid in the Cross Chamber. When Nikon was Patriarch, a table was also laid for beggars and homeless people, and the Patriarch would treat them personally during the repast. Prayers were said, and all guests would first partake of the large Host of Our Lady on a gold-plated silver platter in the middle of the table. Then the guests of honor would be offered a glass of wine, while the Patriarch himself would drink three goblets of wine in their honor. Then bread was served individually for each guest while a stolnik

Sacerdotal robes of Patriarch Nikon, made from Italian silk with embossed gold embroidery

servant shouted out the name, rank, title and diocese of the dignitary being served. Then everyone would eat. Red and black caviar came first, followed by a great variety of fish and seafood dishes. As was the royal custom, dishes would be served in turns, not at the same time. Every time the servants freshened drinks, they would use new goblets of a different shape. It was customary to pack each guest's favorite food for them to take home. Guest servants would immediately take the food packages home with the Patriarch's blessing.

Bratina, Patriarch Nikon's gift to Czar Alexius (1653). Bratina, deriving from the word "brat" (brother) was a bowl to pass around at parties. While drinking, everyone would sing praise to Virgin Mary, so a bratina was also called "Our Lady's Bowl."

A typical menu featured five or six varieties of oukha fish chowder with pies, all kinds of smoked and kippered sturgeon, and telnoe (fish fillets baked in the shape of a goose or lamb with many different spices and with special "lamb" flavor), not to mention pyshki (doughnuts), syrniki (curd cakes), and oladyi (pancakes). When someone drank to the Patriarch, they had to drink down and show that their goblet was empty by turning it over above their head. Then

everyone would drink to the Czar, Czarina, and their children.

During the entire dinner party, a priest at the lectern in the middle of the room would read in a stentorian voice from the life of the saint whose memory happened to be celebrated that day, from time to time superceded by a choir, which the Patriarch and his guests would occasionally join. After the feast, Our Lady's Host was laid out in the middle of the table once again. Everyone rose, said their prayers, and, as was the monastic custom at the time, rolled the tablecloth together keeping all the bread crumbs and food rejects inside. If the Patriarch dined alone, he would then take a long rest until vespers (4:00 or 5:00 pm). It was also customary in Russia to take a nap after dinner. After vespers, the Russian Patriarch attended to more private matters: he reviewed petitions, read religious books or wrote. The Patriarch would go to bed before midnight, but would sometimes rise and pray in the middle of the night.

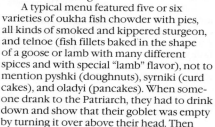

Patriarch Nikon presenting new church books at the 1654 Church Assembly

Poteshny Palace

The low, festive looking building stretching from the Trinity Tower along the Kremlin wall is the Poteshny, or Amusement Palace. In the mid-17th century, chambers were built here for the Boyar leader Ilya Miloslavsky. Czar Alexius, who married Miloslavsky's daughter Maria, gave his father-in-law a plot of land in the Kremlin. Miloslavsky was a hospitable and generous host. At Christmas-tide, Shrove-tide and Easter, the Czar, his family and courtiers would come here for sumptuous dinners, accompanied by live music and occasional drama performances. The Czar enjoyed Miloslavsky's feasts, but he was wary of the excesses, and theatrical performances were frowned on in those times. The Czar would talk to his priest at length every time before attending, and took a bath after each performance to wash off the "theatrical filth." Then he prayed for forgiveness. When Ilya Miloslavsky died in 1668, his house became property of the Czar as Miloslavsky had left no heirs.

During the reign of Feodor, Alexius' son, the Poteshny Palace was renovated and redecorated. The top-floor Terem was reappointed as a house temple — the Church of the Praise of Our Lady with side altars dedicated to St. Alexius the Man of God and St. Mary of Egypt. A proper theater was fashioned inside the palace. At this point, women from the royal family were allowed to come to the theater openly alongside the men. Tatiana Arsenieva, a beautiful Boyar daughter, would star in most performances. Then Princess Sophia with her sisters moved into the Poteshny Palace, so now it was a proper royal palace. For her housewarming, Sophia rehearsed her own play about Catherine the Holy Martyr, which was a resounding success.

In the early 19th century, the Poteshny Palace housed the Kremlin Commandant with his staff, and the former royal chambers became regular offices. The palace retained its historical name, but nothing amusing was going on here anymore. The last traces of humor vanished after 1917, when some serious Bolshevik functionaries moved in. More tragic events unfolded on 9 November 1932. Joseph Stalin's wife Nadezhda Allilueva committed suicide here in a room overlooking Aleksandrovsky Garden.

The palace currently belongs to the Kremlin Commandant's office, and visitors are not allowed anywhere near it. Let this lonely white and yellow toy house reminisce wistfully about its cheerful past, basking in its own reflection in the vast windows of the concrete and glass giant across the way.

View of the Poteshny Palace

State Kremlin Palace

The State Kremlin Palace, a bulky concrete and glass structure, was erected in 1961 as a Congress Palace to the order of Nikita Khrushchev. Although originally intended for Communist Party

This monumental Palace was very artfully blended into the Kremlin's centuries-old architectural landscape

conventions, this multipurpose building has also seen music concerts, ballet, opera, and other performances over the years. Incidentally, the new Congress Palace was

the reason why UNESCO did not put all of the Kremlin on its World Heritage List. Only Cathedral Square was included as an architectural complex that has retained its historic integrity.

Before 1917, there was a barracks building where the Kremlin Palace now stands, housing the Ekaterinoslavsky Regiment of Kremlin guards. According to contemporaries, during the reign of Alexander I the barracks' façade was decked with stucco moldings depicting scenes from Russian history, and statues of prominent people who had served Russia well. The decorations wore off over time, and were removed. After remodeling, the barracks building looked hardly more remarkable than today's side wall of the Congress Palace.

In some way, the State Kremlin Palace is like an iceberg, and not only because it looks like a cold, white chunk if ice. Similarly to an iceberg, the bulk of this structure is hidden as deep as 15 meters underground. The building has over 800 rooms, including a 6,000 seat conference room with an enormous stage. Today, the palace is better known as Moscow's most prestigious performance venue.

The main foyer of the State Kremlin Palace

Arsenal

Arsenal

Across from the State Kremlin Palace is the Arsenal, founded by Peter I to replace the former Strelets compound, where the Strelets guards, backed by Princess Sophia, had plotted a conspiracy against the Czar in 1689. According to other evidence, there had never been a conspiracy, and Sophia claimed to have been falsely accused. But this notwithstanding, all the buildings here were pulled down. The construction of the Arsenal (or "Zeichhaus" as Peter I preferred to call it) was repeatedly interrupted by wars and fires. The Arsenal emerged in its present shape after a 1828 remodeling.

Ancient cannons at the Arsenal

In the early 1900s, military trainees came for marching practice to the plaza in front of the Arsenal, which housed weapons and ammunition inside. The Arsenal has long since lost its role as a military depot, and currently houses the Presidential Regiment, which guards the Kremlin. Its soldiers also serve as guards of honor at various ceremonies, where they wear their ceremonial outfits with headgear shaped like shako hats from the 1812 Franco-Russian War.

But the Arsenal can still be viewed as a military memorial, standing above hundreds of military trophies: cannons seized from French soldiers were hauled here en masse starting November 1812. Back then, cannons were considered equal to enemy flags in symbolic importance as trophies.

When Napoleon's own troops captured a massive amount of cannons in the Battle of Austerlitz, he ordered them smelted to cast the Vendome Column of Triumph, which still adorns Paris. 875 cannons lie at the foot of the Arsenal, 365 of them French-made, and the rest captured by Napoleon elsewhere, and then seized by Russians from his army.

View of the Arsenal

The Senate

The Senate, the supreme legislative advisory body of the Russian Empire, was established by Peter I in 1711. Over time, the Senate lost some of its significance, turning into the supreme judicial authority. The main seat of the Senate was in St. Petersburg, but Catherine II transferred two Senate departments to Moscow. Matvei Kazakov, the most celebrated architect of the day, built a luxurious building for the Senators at the Kremlin in 1776–1787. The unusual triangular shape of the building was dictated by the need to match the surrounding landscape of the old Chudov and Voznesensky Monasteries. There is an architectural lesson to be learned here, and a case of poetic injustice. The sacred monasteries were demolished without a trace in the 1930s, and some barracks were built instead, as if mocking the architect's hard work.

The chief decoration of the Senate building is its dome above St. Catherine Hall. They say that on the day the palace was delivered for occupancy, Kazakov climbed on top of the dome to prove the structure (which was fairly unusual for Moscow) was solid.

In the late 19th century, the building was renamed "Litigation Building," and was, essentially, a large law firm. The building changed hands in March 1918, when the Sovnarkom (the government of the early Soviet republic) moved in. A study and apartment for its chairman, Vladimir Lenin, were appointed on the third (top) floor. From then on, the Senate became the most significant government building. These walls remember many Soviet leaders and dramatic events. In 1990 the Senate building became the residence of Mikhail Gorbachev, the first and last President of the Soviet Union,

The main entrance of the Senate

who would officially resign here in front of a host of TV cameras only a year later. The red Soviet flag was removed from the top of Kazakov's dome, and the Russian tricolor went up.

More recently, the historical building has been assigned a new role again — it is now the principal residence of the President of Russia. The building underwent massive interior remodeling in the mid-1990s. (An empty secret hiding place was accidentally discovered under Stalin's former office). The obsolete, wood paneled offices were transformed into luxury suites. New additions to the building include some galleries, official reception rooms, beautiful fireplaces, chandeliers, and fancy, expensive furniture. This is now a presidential palace, and some parts of it are familiar to us from TV. The interiors in the palace were also designed by Ilya Glazunov.

This room looks quite modest, with some engravings on the walls; this wall is draped in red fabric with numerous golden double eagles; these beautiful halls are lined with portraits: we recognize Alexander I in

In 1918 the resident quaters of Vladimir Lenin was arranged in the Senate

Interior of the St. Catherine Hall

eclecticism in the decorations, producing an ambiguous impression. And, finally, the official room painted in white and green hues — the venue of summit meetings and talks. The features catching one's eye here are the heavy curtains, the malachite fireplace with a huge clock, and white, green-upholstered Italian furniture. But the chief attraction here are the tall sculptures of four Russian monarchs: Peter I, Catherine II, Nicholas I and Alexander II, standing there as symbols of historic succession of power, and a reminder of the fact the reform is essential to successful governance.

And yet the spherical St. Catherine Hall right underneath the dome remains the most magnificent and the best known place in the Senate building, admired for its Classicist perfection for two centuries. Its white and blue, sunlit space is decked with gold-plated double eagles and allegorical female statues of Russia and Justice in the niches. More allegoric statues — this time gigantic ones — line the main entrance to the inner patio. The main entrance is near the St. Nicholas Tower. On the small dome above the gate is an image of St. George with a spear on horseback, a reminder of the similar sculpture that used to stand on top of the building in the 18th century before the presidential flag took its place.

black uniform and cocked hat, and that's Nicholas I... All the interiors are evocative of the late Empire, the style of the Alexander II era. And here is the holy of holies of Russian statehood — the President's study, where moderate austerity is combined with some

In the Heraldic Hall of the Senate Palace the President receives the ambassadors of foreign nations

ARCEC Military School

Many centuries ago, Moscow's oldest monasteries — Chudov (Miracle) and Voznesensky (Ascension), as well as the Maly St. Nicholas Palace — stood by the Kremlin's Spasskie (Savior's) Gate. (Read about them in the chapter on Lost Landmarks of the Kremlin). In 1918, the Soviet government moved from St. Petersburg (then Petrograd) to Moscow and settled in the Kremlin, ordering all monasteries closed. In 1929, the government decided to pull them down. In 1932–1934, a military school was built here, named after the All Russia Central Executive Committee [of the Communist Party] (ARCEC) — the supreme legislative, decision-making and controlling government body in the Soviet Union between 1917 and 1936. At the time, the ARCEC was chaired by well-known Soviet political figures: Lev Kamenev, Yakov Sverdlov and Mikhail Kalinin. The ARCEC school became the Soviet Union's first military educational institution to train career officers.

The former military school is laid out like a trident pointed at the Senate building. Its main façade faces the Moskva River. The other façade faces Ivanovskaya (St. John) Square. From 1938 on, the building housed the Supreme Council of the USSR until 1958, when

The Conference Hall of the present-day administrative building

a part of it was remodeled to house the 1200 seat Kremlin Theater that only lasted until 1961. In a further remodeling project, a part of the building was converted to Marble Hall, the place for official government functions. This is where the President of Russia delivers his annual address to the Federal Assembly.

The building currently houses the Office of the President and the Kremlin Commandant's Office. Public access to the building is restricted.

The former Military School has been turned into administrative building

The Great Imperial Crown, the Small Imperial Crown, the Scepter and the Orb

Diamond Depository

The Kremlin's Diamond Depository dates back to the reign of Peter I, who decreed for the most valuable treasures to become property of the Russian state, not only of the Royal Family. From then on, precious regalia, insignia and secular jewelry belonging to several generations of Russian rulers would be stored in the Diamond Room in St. Petersburg until 1914. When WWI broke out, the collection was moved to Moscow and placed in the Armory basement, where it would stay for nearly 8 years. The Diamond Depository was established in 1922, but only in 1967, when the Soviet state was celebrating its 50th anniversary, were the treasures placed on public display.

The Order of St. Andrew, the oldest Order of Russia

Russia's Diamond Depository is an assemblage of precious stones, jewelry, rare gold and platinum nuggets of tremendous historical and monetary value and creative merit. The collection features seven gems, known as "historic," that have no match anywhere else in the world.

The famous Orlov diamond (189.62 karats) on a gold royal scepter was already described in the chapter Cathedral of the Assumption: Ascending the Throne.

A giant dark-red spinel (398.72 karats) adorns the Great Imperial Crown, with which all Russian monarchs, from Catherine II to Nicholas II, were crowned. Royal envoy Nicholas Spapharius bought this fiery, shimmering stone in China in 1676 under orders from Czar Alexius, the father of Peter I. The Chinese seller, a nobleman of distinction, asked Spapharius to keep the deal a secret, otherwise he could have faced the death sentence for letting such a treasure leave China.

A big Colombian emerald (136.25 karats) of the purest dark green hue is inserted in a brooch that once belonged to Empress Elizabeth, the wife of Alexander I. Speculating about the gem's provenance, Soviet

The Diamond Depository is located in the same building as the Armory

Gold bracelet with the world's largest flat diamond

historian Fersman wrote: "It must have been found during the Middle Ages, at the time America was discovered. In all likelihood, the Portuguese had removed it from a native temple in Colombia. Then the stone somehow made it to India, where it blended in with local emeralds. It was always a mystery how valuable treasures from Oriental treasure-troves and harems ended up in European antique shops, but one day this gem, too, made its way to Europe."

The world's largest flat diamond (weight 25 karat, surface 7.5 square cm), embedded in a gold bracelet, also belonged to Empress Elizabeth. Instead of glass, the stone covers a miniature watercolor portrait of Alexander I on ivory, replicating the gem's shape.

One of the largest in the world, the Ceylon cut sapphire (260.37 karat), shining from a diamond-encrusted gold brooch, was purchased by Alexander II from an Indian raja at the 1862 Grand London Expo as a present for his wife, Empress Maria. "It pales the famous Rospoli in Paris, and even the legendary sapphire of the Duke of Devonshire," Fersman wrote.

This unique chrysolite (192.6 karat) from the Red Sea Island of Zaberget came to Russia in the 19th century. According to legend, it had belonged to Byzantine emperors before Byzantium was looted by the Crusaders in the early 13th century. Russian jewelers gave it a set of vintage cut diamonds in 1985.

The seventh 'historic' stone and one of the best-known gems in the world is the Shah diamond (88.7 karat), found in the 16th century in the mines of Golconda, an early Indian state. It belonged to the Great Moguls, rulers of India and Afghanistan. According to legend, it was a Mogul talisman hanging above the throne on a silk thread. After the Great Moguls were defeated by the Persians in the 18th century, the diamond became property of Nadir, the Shah of Persia. The names of its successive owners are engraved in Arabic on the stone, which was believed to bring its owner great strength and power. After Alexander Griboedov, the Russian ambassador to Persia and also a great diplomat and writer, was assassinated in Tehran in 1829, the Shah sent lavish gifts to Emperor Nicholas I to defuse an international conflict. The stone was among those gifts, and was named 'Shah' in honor of the giver.

Breastplate with a gold-set, diamond-encrusted image of Peter I (early 18th century). The Emperor awarded it personally for exceptional service to the homeland.

In the 1922 collection, 40% of items were from the reign of Catherine II. Wearing a floral diamond brooch, a diadem, and large earrings with floral ornaments, the Empress dressed up as Flora, the Goddess of Flowers, for one of the royal fancy dress balls. A thin layer of multicolored tinfoil gives the translucent diamonds rose, tulip and camomile hues. The gold leaves are covered with green enamel. Diamond bees are sitting, as if frozen,

Victory Order No. 1 was awarded to Marshal Georgy Zhukov in 1944.

on the petals of the diadem and earrings.

The depository was considerably enlarged with diamonds from Yakutia during the decades of Soviet rule. In line with the tradition, they were all given names like "26th Congress of the Communist Party" (342 karats), "60 Years of Komsomol" (200.7 karats), "Soviet Constitution" (119.6 karats). Some diamonds were also named in honor of the first astronaut, Yuri Gagarin, and the first female astronaut, Valentina Tereshkova. A large diamond was named "Free Russia" (242 karats) in the 1990s.

The collection also features valuable Russian and international insignia. The diamond symbol and star of the Order of the Holy Apostle Andrew the First Called is believed to have belonged to Peter I, who established this first Russian order in 1698 for distinguished military leaders. Peter himself was the sixth person to win it for the capture of two Swedish warships in the Neva delta. The typical awards in early Russia were things like gold and silver ladles, luxurious furs, royal caftans or fur coats. Russia's first 'female' order of St. Catherine, shaped as a gold medallion, was established by Peter to celebrate his army's fortunate deliverance from a very dangerous military situation in 1711, when Peter I and his army were surrounded by Turkish troops, who outnumbered the Russians five times over. Skillful negotiations, coupled with some lavish gifts sent by Peter's wife Catherine to the Turkish commander convinced the Turks to conclude an armistice.

The collection includes some Soviet insignia as well, most notably the Marshal Star and the Victory

This decoration, named Grand Bouquet (16 x 21 cm, ca. 1760), is made from gold, silver, Brazilian diamonds and Colombian emeralds. The slightest motion makes its leaves and flowers shake

Order. Established for Soviet Marshals in 1940, the Marshal star is a five-pointed star with diamonds embedded between the points, and another platinum, diamond-encrusted star in the middle. The standard Victory Order is a five-pointed platinum star with diamond-encrusted ruby points. Established in 1943, the order was awarded to 11 highest-ranking military commanders during WWII.

The gold and platinum nugget collection is centered around the exhibits from the St. Petersburg Mining Institute, transferred to Moscow after 1917. Some gold nuggets are named according to their shape: "Dolphin" (10 kg), "Camel" (9.3 kg), and the tiniest one, "Mephistopheles" (20.25 g), a true miracle of nature. The "Rabbit Ears" nugget (3.3 kg) from the Urals contains 93.2% of pure gold. It was found by the roadside in 1935.

The platinum nugget called "Ural Giant," weighing around 8 kg, is one of the largest in the world. Unlike gold nuggets, platinum nuggets are much rarer, and their shape is usually lumpy and boring. There was no use for platinum until the 18th century, so platinum nuggets were thrown away as useless rocks. Not anymore.

The "Great Triangle" is the world's largest gold nugget weighing 36.2 kg, mined in the Urals in 1842

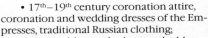

Treasures of the Armory

Founded by Great Prince Vasily III in the early 16th century, the Armory was originally a workshop manufacturing military equipment for combat and parades. In the 17th century, the first Romanov rulers had the Armory expanded, making it the largest artisan's shop in the Kremlin. The best Russian gunsmiths, jewelers and icon painters worked here side by side with their international counterparts from Germany, Poland and elsewhere in Eastern Europe.

Peter I ordered active manufacturing operations moved to the new capital — St. Petersburg, while the Kremlin Armory remained a depository of old military and church artifacts. The Armory had no building of its own, so the exhibits were constantly moved around until Alexander I upgraded the Armory's status to an Imperial Museum, and ordered a building erected for it by the Troitskie Gate, where the State Kremlin Palace now stands.

Emperor Nicholas I personally contributed to the design of the existing Armory, which was at that point viewed as the Romanov Family museum since many of its original exhibits

The large and heavy purse (called "kalita" in old Russian), which Great Prince Ivan Kalita always carried around on his belt.

had been stolen or looted during the "Time of Troubles" in 1605–1612. Opened in 1851, the Armory became Moscow's first public museum of history.

The Armory currently features some four thousand exhibits, spanning the 12th through early 20th centuries.

The exhibits include:
- Russian and foreign military equipment and trophies;
- church relics from Kremlin churches and the Patriarch's Sacristy;
- ambassadorial and other gifts to Moscow Czars, Czarinas, and Emperor Alexander I;
- Russian Imperial regalia, royal crowns and garments;

- 17th–19th century coronation attire, coronation and wedding dresses of the Empresses, traditional Russian clothing;
- silver goblets and other royal tableware; everyday items with the images of Peter I and Russian Empresses;
- items from the Stables Office: parade outfits for horses, created by Russian and foreign tailors, historical carriages, tapestries and trellises;
- other unique artifacts.

Remarkable exhibits at the Armory
(only a few of a great number of historical and religious artifacts are listed; the figures indicate window numbers)

2nd floor, Room #1
Room #1 showcases the earliest sacred artifacts from 14th–17th century Kremlin churches, historical Russian jewelry and tableware from the 11th–12th centuries, as well as objects of Byzantine, southern Slavonic and Georgian applied art.

1. St. Dmitrius of Solun icon in stone (talc), 11th century. The Emperor of Byzantium is believed to have sent the icon to Prince Dmitry Donskoy on the occasion of Russia's victory at Kulikovo Field.

2. A Russian tabernacle (1383) with the holy gifts Dionysus the Archbishop of Suzdal brought back from Constantinople. Shoulder barmas (symbols of princely or royal highness) and kolty (headdress pendants) from the Ryazan Treasury (12th century). Eucharist chalice believed to have been created to the order of Prince Yuri Dolgoruky, the founder of Moscow.

3. The Gospel on parchment (1415) inside an exquisite jewel-encrusted gold frame, believed to have been created by an artist of the Andrei Rubliov circle.

4. Gold-plated silver frame for a hand-written Gospel (1499), a gift to the Church of the Assumption from Metropolitan Simon. Two tabernacles shaped like Orthodox churches — the Bolshoi and Maly Zion (1486): they were brought out for special divine services.

Window #3. The frame of the miracle-working Icon of Our Lady of Vladimir (14ᵗʰ–15ᵗʰ centuries), crafted using the basma technique (hand stamping on a gold background)

Window #4. Another gold frame for the Icon of Our Lady of Vladimir (15ᵗʰ century)

7. Church artifacts Ivan the Terrible took from Novgorod churches: The Gospel in a silver filigreed frame, a gold-plated silver chalice, and others (16ᵗʰ century).

8. The gold-plated silver shrine lids of to St. Czarevich Dmitry (from the Cathedral of the Archangel Michael (1630) and St. Cyril Belozersky (from the St. Cyril Belozersky Monastery (1643).

Room #2

In this room, like the first one, of particular interest are the sundry fascinating artifacts from the Kremlin's historical churches, as well as the legendary Faberge Easter eggs.

5. Gold artifacts from the Cathedral of the Archangel Michael, donated by Czarina Irina Godunova: a church-shaped censer, small tabernacle and chalice. The gold plate was Ivan the Terrible's wedding gift to his second wife Maria Temriukovna (1561).

6. Ivan the Terrible's panagia (an icon to wear round the neck) with the image of his celestial patron, St. John the Precursor as the Angel of the Wilderness, on a blue sardonix (16ᵗʰ century). The Gospel in a jewel-encrusted gold frame (1571): Ivan the Terrible's gift to the Cathedral of the Annunciation. Framed icon of St. John Climacus, or St. John of the Ladder (1554), sized to the measure of the infant Czarevich John, Ivan the Terrible's son. Folding icon of St. Nicholas the Miracle-Worker (16ᵗʰ century) that once belonged to the wife of Czarevich Ivan, Alexandra Saburova, whom Ivan the Terrible ordered sent to a convent soon after the wedding.

9. Objects from the sacristy of the Troitse-Sergieva Lavra: the gold censer (1616) and gold-framed Gospel (1632) were gifts from Czar Mikhail and Patriarch Philaret; The Gospel that belonged to Prince Dmitry Pozharsky (1613); the frame for the Trinity icon (16ᵗʰ–17ᵗʰ centuries) from the Ipatievsky Monastery in Kostroma was a gift from Dmitry Godunov, the uncle of Boris Godunov.

10. 17ᵗʰ century gold and silver utensils: solid gold scoops and goblets that belonged to Czar Mikhail; bratina (brotherhood) mead bowls (bratina bowls full of mead were passed around in a circle, so everyone had a drink), and others. The wife of Deacon Piotr Tretyakov presented Czar Mikhail with one of these bratina bowls in 1618 together with a pardon plea for her husband, who stood accused of high treason. There is an

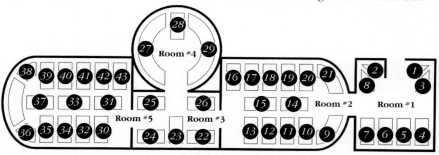

2nd floor plan of the Armory

engraved inscription on the edge of the bowl: "True love is like a vessel of gold; it can never break, and if it bends a little here and there, it is easy to fix."

11. The gold-framed Gospel encrusted with rubies and amethysts from the sacristy of the Chudov Monastery was a gift from Czar Alexius (1668). These cutlery holders belonged to Peter I and Czarina Sophia.

12. Hand-made items from Solvychegodsk: sacred images, tableware and chests crafted using a proprietary color enamel technique (17th century).

13. Gold-plated silver church objects from the churches of Kostroma, Yaroslavl and other Volga towns: chalices, censers, incense holders, and others (17th century).

14. The Gospel from the sacristy of the Verkhospassky Cathedral of the Terem Palace was a gift from Czar Feodor (1678); the chalice from the sacristy of the Chudov Monastery was a gift from Boyarynya Morozova (1664).

15. Jewelry with images of Peter I (a badge and a snuffbox), and a panagia that may have belonged to Stephen Jaworski, the first President of the Holiest Synod (early 17th century).

16. A gold tabernacle crafted in Moscow (1753). Gold and silver artifacts made by

Russian craftsmen in the 18th century, including Elizabeth's snuffbox – a gift from Count Aleksei Razumovsky (1759).

17. Carved gold and silver objects from Veliky Ustiug and Tobolsk: the Tobolsk Governor's tea set, snuffboxes, and other artifacts (13th–19th centuries).

18. Prince Grigory Potiomkin's gold plate, on which he received a diamond-encrusted sword from Catherine II in gratitude for the conquest of the fortress of Ochakov (1788). Two children's tea sets were gifts from Catherine II to her grandchildren: Czareviches Alexander and Constantine. The Gospel (1698) in a frame of gold, silver and jewels (1794).

19. The wedding wreaths that, according to legend, Alexander Pushkin and Natalia Goncharova wore at their wedding ceremony in 1831.

20. On display here are precious panagias from the Patriarch's sacristy, and Faberge Easter eggs. One egg contains the mechanical replica of an East Siberian Railway train (1900). Another one, dedicated to the 300th anniversary of the House of Romanov, contains a revolving steel globe with two gold images of the Northern Hemisphere, where Russia's borders are marked as they were in 1613 and 1913.

21. Russian gold-plated silverware and sculptures (19th – early 20th centuries).

Window #6. An egg shaped like a Kremlin replica with a music box (1904); the egg itself is shaped like the dome of the Cathedral of the Assumption with iconostasis inside

Room #3
Room #3 comes after Room #4 on the tour, containing 15th–19th century oriental and European parade weaponry and equipment.

22, 23, 24. Suits of armor, swords and firearms from Germany, France

Window #14. Czar Alexius I's plate (1653)

Window #20. Panagia with diamonds and red tourmalines: a gift from Catherine II to Plato, the Metropolitan of Moscow (1775).

The Armory's Silver Room in the 19th century (left) and today

and elsewhere in Western Europe (15th–19th centuries).

25, 26. Iranian and Turkish parade armor; swords with Arabic inscriptions, and other weapons: gifts to Czar Alexius from Istanbul and Constantinople merchants and the Shah of Persia (16th–17th centuries).

Room #4

An openwork iron Heraldic lattice with the coats of arms of the earliest towns, principalities and lands of the Russian Empire separates the Round Room, which contains 12th to 19th century Russian weaponry and 17th to 20th century Russian military awards. The majority of these exhibits belonged to eminent military leaders and statesmen.

27. This helmet, the earliest of all, belonged to Prince Yaroslav, the father of Alexander Nevsky (early 13th century); Yaroslav wore it to the 1216 battle between Novgorodians and Suzdalians, where his troops were defeated. He hid his helmet and armor in the ground and fled. A peasant woman found the helmet and rusty armor under a tree in 1808. 16th century suit of armor that belonged to Prince Peter Shuisky, Ivan the Terrible's warlord. When the prince died, Ivan the Terrible gave it to Ermak, the conqueror of Siberia. Minin's and Prince Pozharsky's swords. This gold saadak (sheath for bow and arrows, 1628) was part of the official outfit of Czar Mikhail along with the scepter and the orb.

28. A 17th century Russian warrior with full parade works on horseback.

29. Trophies from the Battle of Poltava: Swedish weaponry, horns and drums, personal belongings of King Karl XII, including his Bible, etc. Collected Russian military awards established in the 18th century: Orders of the Holy Apostle Andrew the First-Called, St. Alexander Nevsky, St. Anna, St. George the Victorious, and St. Prince Vladimir.

Room #5

This is the last room on the 2nd floor, featuring 13th to 19th century European silver objects. Most of them were gifts to Moscow Czars from foreign ambassadors: silverware, goblets, washstands, and other utensils. The Czars usually reciprocated with more generous gifts. It was customary for the Patriarch, monasteries, courtiers of distinction, boyars and merchants to give the Czars such gifts as goblets, plates and chalices

Window #27. Czar Mikhail's formal helmet which, according to legend, had previously belonged to Alexander Nevsky.

on their Name Day and on special occasions. This standard clock was crafted by David Roentgen, purveyor to the court of Ludwig XVI, purchased by Catherine II.

30, 31, 32, 33, 34. Gifts from the embassies of Holland, England, Poland, Sweden and Denmark (16th–17th centuries).

35. Silver goblets from Nuremberg (16th–17th centuries). The goblet shaped like a bunch of grapes was Boris Godunov's gift to Iov, the first Russian Patriarch, on the occasion of his ordainment as Patriarch.

36. 13th–16th century artifacts from Europe: Ivan Kalita period chalice (Florence, 1330); Ivan III's rooster goblet (Germany, 15th century); goblet that belonged to Matthias I, the King of Hungary (1488), and others.

Dutch silver decanter: a gift to Czar Alexius (1665)

37. Outlandish goblets, glasses, vases, and artifacts made from seashells, bones and other natural material, framed in gold and silver (16th–17th centuries).

38. 16th–19th century European jewelry.

39. 17th century gold-plated silver jewelry from Hamburg.

40. The world's largest collection of gold-plated silver objects from Augsburg, Germany: 17th to 18th century goblets, plates, candleholders, etc.

41. 17th–18th century French silverware, including items from the Orlov set (1770–1771) – a gift from Catherine II to Count Grigory Orlov; the set, numbering more than

3000 items, was intended for 40 persons; it took over two tons of silver to make.

42. Napoleon-era French silverware (early 19th century Empire).

43. The "Olympic" porcelain set from the French town of Sevres (early 19th century) features 140 items with scenes from the life of mythical Greek gods and heroes – the denizens of Olympus. Not a single scene is repeated twice. The set was Napoleon's gift to Alexander I in 1807, when the Tilsit peace treaty was signed.

1st floor, Room #6

This room contains the Russian Czars' ceremonial dress, sacerdotal robes of the first Russian Orthodox Patriarchs, gold, silver and pearl embroidered garments of courtiers, headdress of Moscow Czarinas and Princesses, precious fabrics and ornamental embroidery from the 15th through 18th centuries.

44. The wool mantle (coat) of Metropolitan Philip is the oldest exhibit here. He wore this coat in 1568 when he went into exile, having fallen into disfavor with Ivan the Terrible. Ivan the Terrible's staff, the one he used to kick his subjects in moments of extreme wrath, occasionally mutilating them. Czar Mikhail's red satin mantle to wear over the suit of armor. Peter I's clothing: a green satin homespun coat without collar, velvet caftan with a double eagle, European-cut riding caftan, and the jackboots and staff the Emperor made himself.

Treasures of the Armory

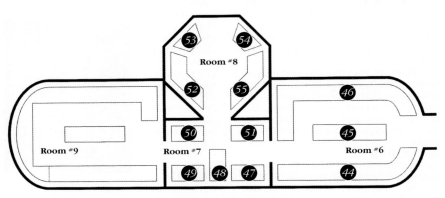

1st floor plan of the Armory

45. Imperial coronation attire: Nicholas II's uniform and Alexandra's dress and ermine mantle — the outfits they wore to their last coronation in 1896. Coronation dresses of Catherine I, Anna, Elizabeth, and Catherine II.

46. Vestments from the Patriarch's Sacristy, including the pearl-embroidered robe Catherine II gave to Plato, the Metropolitan of Moscow, containing over 150,000 pearls.

Room #7

This room displays early Russian state regalia used in coronation and parade ceremonies in the 13th through 18th centuries. Chancellor Hans Cobenzel, envoy of the German Emperor Maximilian II, wrote about his impressions from the Moscow court in 1576: "I've

The artist Viktor Vasnetsov painted Ivan the Terrible with his famous staff, now on display in the Armory

never seen so many rich and beautiful things in one place... and I've seen the crowns and all the vestments of the Catholic King and Grand Prince of Tuscany, and many treasures of the King of France and His Imperial Majesty in the Hungarian Kingdom, in Bohemia and elsewhere. But believe you me: all of this cannot even come close to what I've seen [in Moscow]." The exhibits in Room #7 are described in more detail in the chapter entitled Cathedral of the Assumption: Ascending the Throne.

47, 48, 49. Ivan III-era ivory throne on which, according to legend, Ivan the Terrible was crowned (16th century). Czar Mikhail's throne (17th century), which was used for all coronations including the very last one. Czar Alexius-era diamond throne (1659). Boris Godunov's throne (or "Persian Armchair") (until 1604). Silver double throne of the Czareviches Peter and Alexius (17th century). Empress Elizabeth's throne (1740–1742).

50. The Monomakh Hat, the coronation headdress of the Russian Czars in the

15th–17th centuries. The coronet, orb and scepter from Czar Mikhail's "Grand Attire" (16th–17th centuries); items from the "Grand Attire" of Czar Alexius (1650s). The hat of the Czar of Kazan (16th century). Empress Anna crown (1730s). Paul I's Maltese crown (17th century). The national sword and shield (17th century).

Room #8

Room #8 contains exhibits from the Stables Office, which stood where the Armory is today: horse harnesses (horsecloths, saddles, bridles, etc.), as well as horse attire for formal events, made by foreign craftsmen in the 16th–18th centuries.

52, 53, 54, 55. Horse attire for formal events, made by Russian, Turkish, Iranian and European craftsmen: Czars' and Emperors' saddles, etc.

Room #9

The public display section features 16th–18th century historical carriages, including the English carriage given by King Jacob I as a gift to Boris Godunov (1603). The carriage of Empress Elizabeth (18th century), which she rode from St. Petersburg to Moscow for her coronation. Catherine II's carriage (1763), in which she traveled to the Crimea.

The door of Empress Elizabeth's carriage (Berlin, 1746)

The throne of Empress Elizabeth. 1740-1742

ІС ХС

Св. прєп. Сергій рад. ч. Св. прєп. Варлаал

Walls and Towers of the Kremlin

The 2235 m Kremlin wall traces the outline of the Kremlin Hill, going up and down rather steeply with a difference of nearly four times between the lowest and highest places: from 5 m to 19 m. The wall ranges from 3.5 to 6.5 m in thickness.

A battlement parapet 2 to 4.5 m wide, invisible from the outside, runs atop the entire length of the wall with 1045 two-horned merlons 2 to 2.5 m tall and 65 to 70 cm thick, and with narrow crenels. There are dark, windowless prisoner cells in the hallways inside some of the towers.

Each tower was built with a small gazebo on top with bells that tolled in case of fire or danger. There were cannons on top of the Kremlin wall until the 17th century. Another, lower wall ran some distance outside the existing Kremlin wall.

The Kremlin walls and towers were built in 1485–1499, during the reign of Great Prince Ivan III, by Italian architects Antonio Guilardi, Marco Ruffo, Pietro Antonio Solari and Aloisio da Carcano. None of these architects were related to each other or had the same last name in reality, but in Russia, they all went under the last name "Friazin," which was what Russians called all foreigners during the Middle Ages. The new walls were built a little outside the old walls, which were left standing. Dozens of wooden houses surrounding the Kremlin had to be pulled down to make way for the new walls.

There are 20 towers in the Kremlin wall, the oldest being Tainitskaya (the Secret Tower, built in 1485); the youngest — Czarskaya (the Royal Tower, built in 1680). The three angle towers in the corners are different from the others in shape: two of them are rotund, and one has 16 facets. Some towers are accessible from the ground; others from the wall only. Four towers have gates in them. The Kremlin towers were usually named after the churches that used to stand next to them but no longer exist, or some nearby objects.

Before 1917, two-hour excursions were allowed on the top of the Kremlin wall, subject to the commandant's permission. Excursions started from the Borovitskaya Tower.

← **The Icon of Our Savior (in Russian — Spas) above the main Kremlin Spasskie gate gave it its name. Everyone should take his hat off when walking through the gate**

Borovitskaya Tower
(1490, height: 50.7 m)

The multilevel super-structure with a hipped top was built in the 1680s, when the side turret with a gate was also built

The Borovitskaya Tower, designed by Italian architect Pietro Antonio Solari, was the entrance to the logistical part of the royal estate. The name of the tower, the gate and the nearby churches that no longer exist, came from the wood, or bor, that used to cover this part of the Borovitsky Hill.

Until the 1820s, there was a drawbridge that led to the tower across the Neglinka River. At second floor level, one can still see the apertures through which the hoisting chains went.

From the balcony of the Borovitskaya Tower, pre-1917 visitors could enjoy a breathtaking view of the upper reaches of the Moskva River, the Pashkov House, and the Cathedral of Christ the Savior.

Vodovzvodnaya Tower (Water Tower)
(1488, height: 57.7 m)

The tower received its current name in 1633, when Russia's first water supply system was built here, drawing water from the Moskva River. Czar Michael Romanov paid

In 1856, the Vodovzvodnaya Tower served as a repository for the royal valuables evacuated from St. Petersburg during a flood

several barrels of gold for the water pump, manufactured under the supervision of English engineer Christopher Halloway. For over a hundred years, the water tower pumped water reliably to irrigate the many gardens and parks scattered on the slopes of the Kremlin Hill. The water flowed through lead pipes, as no one was aware of the harmful properties of lead at the time.

In 1805, the old tower, which was about to collapse, was dismantled to the foundation, and reconstructed in 1807. In 1812, it was blown up by the French. The tower was rebuilt in 1816–1819 by the architect Osip Bove with some departures from the original.

Blagoveshchenskaya (Annunciation) Tower
(1488, height: 30.7 m)

The tower, built on an earlier limestone foundation going back to the 14th-century white-stone Kremlin, was a prison during the reign of Ivan the Terrible. Its name came from the Annunciation icon that used to adorn the tower. In the 17th century a small gate was made in the wall next to the Blagoveshchenskaya Tower at the request of the laundresses, who needed a shortcut to the river.

The Blagoveshchenskie gate was walled in in 1813, but traces of it are still visible on the inside of the wall

The turret of Tainitskaya Tower was dismantled in 1930, and the Tainitskie Gate was walled in

Tainitskaya (Secret) Tower
(1485, height: 38.4 m)

This was the first structure built by the Italian architect Antonio Guilardi for the southern Kremlin wall. There was a draw-well underneath and a secret passage to the Moskva River for emergency water supply

The church of the Annunciation of God's Mother was dismantled in 1932–1933

Blagoveshchenskaya Tower

during a siege. The secret passage gave the tower its name. There used to be a turret in front of the tower.

In 1770–1771, this section of the Kremlin wall was dismantled together with its four towers, in order to make room for a new Kremlin Palace, designed by Vasily Bazhenov. When Catherine II scrapped the expensive project a few years later, the Tainitskaya Tower was restored in its former shape.

1st Bezymiannaya (Nameless) Tower
(1480s, height: 34.15 m)

The tower was used as a gunpowder depot in the 15th and 16th centuries, but the gunpowder exploded during the 1547 fire, destroying the tower and showering half the Kremlin with debris. As has become known recently, the tower was pulled down again in 1771 to make room for Bazhenov's new palace, and then rebuilt again.

2nd Bezymiannaya (Nameless) Tower
(1480s, height: 30.2 m)

This tower has had an unremarkable history. In 1701, there was a gate in it, walled in later.

The hipped tops of both Bezymiannaya Towers were built in the 1680s

It was also pulled down for Bazhenov's new palace project in 1771, but then built back.

Petrovskaya (Peter's) Tower
(1480s, height: 27,15 m)

This tower was destroyed and rebuilt three times in its history. The part of the wall with the tower was first destroyed in 1612, when the Russians besieged the Polish troops entrenched inside the Kremlin. Czar Michael Romanov had the wall and the tower rebuilt.

Vodovzvodnaya Tower

Cathedral of Christ the Savior

View of the Kremlin wall and Moscow in the 19th century

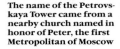

The name of the Petrovskaya Tower came from a nearby church named in honor of Peter, the first Metropolitan of Moscow

The Moskvoretskaya Tower took its name from the Moskvoretsky Bridge nearby

The tower was pulled down in 1771 to make room for Bazhenov's new Kremlin Palace, only to be rebuilt 12 years later. The French blew it up before retreating from Moscow

during the 1812 Russo-French War. Six years later, architect Osip Bove reconstructed the tower in its present shape.

Moskvoretskaya (Moskva River) Tower
(1487, height: 46.2 m)

Architect Marco Ruffo built this tower where the Moskva River met the moat, which used to run along the Kremlin wall facing Red Square. There was a secret place in the basement with special acoustic devices to thwart enemy attempts to dig an underground passage into the Kremlin. The tower was also used as a prison for boyars (nobles) falling foul of the ruler.

Fearing a Swedish invasion, Peter I ordered earthen ramparts built by the tower in 1707 with embrasures for heavy cannons. The embrasures were reconstructed in their original shape in 1949.

Konstantino-Eleninskaya (Sts. Constantine & Helen's) Tower
(1490, height:36.8 m)

Built by the architect Pietro Solari to replace the historical Timofeevskie Gate remaining from the old white-stone

Beklemishevskaya Tower   Petrovskaya Tower   2nd and 1st Bezymiannaya Towers

View of the Kremlin wall and Moscow in the 19th century

The Konstantino-Eleninskaya Tower still bears traces of the gate arch and there's a dent left from the icon case above the gate

The Nabatnaya Tower housed the Spassky fire alarm bell to alert Muscovites

Kremlin, the tower was named after the Kremlin church in honor of St. Constantine and St. Helen, which stood next to it. There used to be a side-turret in front of the tower, connected with it by a bridge. This was the beginning of Velikaya (Great) Ulitsa, the street that ran across the entire

Kitai-Gorod. The gate was walled in in the 17th century, and the turret was converted to a prison and torture chamber for robbers (Constantine's Prison). Horrible rumors circulated about that place.

In 1707, Peter I ordered embrasures made for heavy cannons on the Konstantino-Eleninskaya Tower. The turret and the bridge were later dismantled, and the gate walled in.

Nabatnaya (Alarm Bell) Tower
(1490s, height: 38 m)

In addition to Nabatnaya Tower there were alarm bells on some other towers as well, and their sounds were different. Depending on which bell tolled, Muscovites would know in what part of the city the fire had broken out. During the "plague riots" in Moscow in 1771, rioters broke in the Nabatnaya Tower, and started ringing the bell, calling for further disturbances. After the riots were suppressed, Catherine II ordered the bell punished as the instigator. The bell's tongue was taken out, and it remained silent for 30 years. When the tower was repaired in 1803, the bell was taken down and deposited in the Kremlin Arsenal, and later transferred to the Armory.

A side-turret by the Tainitskaya Tower was dismantled in 1930

The small, elegant Czarskaya Tower stands apart from the others with its unusual shape, looking like a fairy house

Czarskaya (Royal) Tower
(1680, height with weathervane: 16.7 m)

This tower was preceded by a smaller wooden tower, rumored to have been built for Ivan the Terrible so that he could watch the Cathedral of the Intercession being built, and prisoners being executed. It is also a fact that the tower once housed the Spassky fire alarm bells.

Spasskaya (Savior's) Tower and Gate
(1491, height with star: 71 m)

The Kremlin's dominant tower stands tall above the main gate, which once was an object of worship in its own right, called "Holy Gate."

Having annexed Smolensk to the Moscow Principality in 1514, Basil III ordered the Smolensk Icon of the Our Gracious Savior placed on the tower front facing Red Square.

The Kremlin side of the gate displayed a copy of the celebrated Kiev-Pechory Icon of God's Mother, a much worshipped Virgin Mary icon in Kiev Russia. Until 1448, all Russian religious leaders bore the title "Metropolitan of Kiev and All Russia," and the same title was inscribed on their official seals.

In 1648, Czar Alexius issued a decree ordering everyone "forever and ever" to take their hats off when walking through the gate, and posting guards at the gate to make sure everyone

did. Those who forgot to take their hat off were penalized with 50 bows to the ground while crossing themselves and repenting their sins.

The gate bears two memorial plaques — the oldest in Moscow — with inscriptions. On the outside, there is an inscription in Latin, and on the inside, in Russian, both saying that the tower was built by Pietro Solari

The tower is 10 stories tall. The floors from the 7th to 9th house the giant movement of the Spasskaya chiming clock; the 10th floor houses the bells

in 1491 when Grand Prince Ivan III ruled. Interestingly, illiterate people believed the Latin inscription on the gate front was a damnation to anyone daring to enter the Kremlin with their hat on. Up until Peter I's reign, there was a box outside the gate where anyone could drop a petition addressed to the Czar. Russian Czars and then Emperors from Mikhail Romanov to the last Emperor, Nicholas II, passed through the gate on their way to coronation.

The original tower was rectangular and only half the height of the existing one. In 1624–1625, Russian architect Bazhen Ogurtsov teamed up with his English colleague Christopher Halloway to build the tower up with a multistory top, crowned with a hipped roof and a clock.

The French put a gunpowder charge underneath the Spasskie Gate in 1812, but then it suddenly

View of the Spasskaya Tower in the 19th century

The key to the Spasskie Gate with the monogram of Emperor Nicholas I, made in 1833

started raining, and the fire never reached the gunpowder: the fuse went out.

An enormous 17th century treasure was found underneath the gate when workers were digging a ditch there in 1939: 34,769 silver coins, 23 pieces of silver jewelry, and three large pearls in two copper containers. The silver jewelry included earrings with almandine, sapphire, pearl and colored glass pendants. Whoever had hidden 12 kg of treasures in this lively pedestrian area was a very creative thinker.

Spasskaya chiming clock

The earliest clock was installed under orders from Czar Mikhail Romanov to observe church time. The clock dial consisted of 17 sections with old church Slavonic letter-figures and a starry sky in the middle, revolving underneath a static sun with rays, one of which served as a clock hand, marking the hour. According to church rules, the clock struck every hour starting at sunrise, and was switched to night time after sunset. In summer, the clock struck 17 hours during daytime, and 7 hours at night, and this order was reversed in winter.

When, by Peter I's decree, Russia switched to the 24-hour day, the old clock was replaced with a larger Dutch chiming clock with music and our habitual 12-hour dial in 1706–1707. It took 30 horse-drawn carts to deliver the clock to Moscow. The German technicians repairing the clock mischievously made it play the German tune Ah, mein lieber Augustin.

In 1770, the Dutch curiosity was replaced with an English-made chiming clock, which was fully renovated by the Butenop brothers in the mid-19th century, acquiring the look it has today.

Until 1917, the clock chimed the tune of the anthem, Glory to Our Lord in Zion, and Preobrazhensky March. In the Russian Empire, Glory to Our Lord was played during church ceremonies involving troops. In October 1917, during revolutionary upheaval the clock was damaged. Mechanic Nikolai Berents and musician Mikhail Cheremnykh, who repaired the clock in 1920, set it to play L'Internationale

The famous chiming clock. Everything included, the timepiece weighs around 25 tons. The movement is powered by three weights of between 160 kg and 224 kg. Accuracy is assured by a 36 kg pendulum

at noon, and You Perished Like Heroes in the Battle of Doom, at midnight. The tunes were replaced with bell chimes in 1932. Today, the clock chimes the Russian national anthem at noon and midnight.

Senatskaya (Senate) Tower
(1490s, height: 34.3 m)

This tower, built for fortification purposes: to protect the Red Square side of the Kremlin, had no name for a long time before the architect Matvei Kazakov built the Senate in 1787. A rectangular hipped roof was built on the tower in the 1680s.

The Senate dome that can be seen behind the tower was topped by a gold-plated sculpture of St. George the Victorious, Moscow's patron saint, until 1812, when it was toppled by Napoleon's soldiers. It was later replaced with a pillar, topped by a crown as a symbol of the law. Today the dome is crowned by the Russian presidential tricolor flag with a gold-embroidered national emblem of Russia

Nikolskaya (St. Nicholas) Tower and Gate

(1491, height with star: 70.4 m)

The name of this tower derives from the St. Nicholas the Senior Monastery at Nikolskaya Ulitsa nearby, later transformed into a Greek St. Nicholas Monastery.

When the tower was built in the late 15ᵗʰ century, it had a fresco of St. Nicholas the Miracle-Worker with a church in one hand and a sword in the other, surrounded by the archangels, over the gate. Retreating from Moscow, the French blew up the tower in 1812, but the part with the icon survived: the glass on its case didn't even crack. The tower was restored by Osip Bove four years later.

In the 16ᵗʰ through 17ᵗʰ centuries, the Nikolskaya Tower gate led to the boyar and monastery estates inside the Kremlin. Now it is a staff entrance to the Kremlin

Arsenalnaya (Arsenal) Angle Tower

(1492, height: 60.2 m)

This tower, named after the Arsenal when it was built in the early 18ᵗʰ century, originally housed an artesian well that supplied the Kremlin with water before a water supply system was built in the 17ᵗʰ century to draw water from the Moskva River. Some time in the 16ᵗʰ century, someone had hidden valuable military equipment — two helmets and four stirrups, wrapped in a suit of armor — in the above-ground part

The sixteen-faceted Arsenalnaya Angle Tower

of the well. The lavishly decorated helmets suggest that the equipment had belonged to a warrior of distinction. The treasure was found in 1976, more than four centuries later, by a worker cleaning the well.

There was an underground tunnel leading to the Neglinnaya River underneath the tower, filled in later. Over the centuries, numerous attempts were made to find Ivan the Terrible's library, allegedly hidden in the tunnel. The Alexandrovsky Garden, behind a historical wrought-iron fence with gold-plated ornaments, is to the right of the tower.

Sredniaya (Middle) Arsenalnaya Tower

(1495, built up in 1680, height: 38.9 m)

Originally called "faceted," the tower received its present name after the Arsenal was built in the early 18ᵗʰ century. When the Alexandrovsky Garden was planted in 1821, a romantic grotto was built at the foot of the tower, as was the architectural fashion at the time.

View of the Sredniaya Arsenalnaya Tower

Troitskaya (Trinity) Tower and Gate

(1495–1499, height with star: 80 m)

The Troitskie Gate is the main entrance to the Kremlin.

The tower was named in 1658 after the church of Troitse-Sergieva Lavra (Holy Trinity

The main entrance to the Kremlin nowadays is through the Kutafya Tower (on the front) and the gate of Troitskaya Tower (on the rear)

and St. Sergius Monastery) in the Kremlin. The Troitskie Gate was considered second in importance to the Spasskie Gate. In the 17th century, it led to the Czarina's and Princesses' chambers and the Patriarch's estate. In 1612, it was here that the infamous impostor government, consisting of noble traitors and Polish invaders, surrendered to Prince Pozharsky's home guard, and was marched out of the gate.

There used to be a chiming clock on the top level, chiming God Save the Czar. The clock was never restored after the 1812 fire.

The tower has six stories and deep two-level basements, which were used as prison cells in the 16th and 17th centuries. The tower housed the archives of the Imperial Court Ministry until the 1917 revolution.

Kutafya Tower
(1516)

The stone bridge with the Kutafya Tower at the end was built over the Neglinka River, which flowed here, in 1516. In 1685, the tower was decorated with an ornamental top. This is the Kremlin's only surviving bridge tower, protecting a fortress bridge. There used to be a moat in front of the tower with draw-bridges over it. The slits for the hoisting chains are still visible by the side gate. It is believed that the tower's name derived from the old Russian word "kut," or "corner".

Komendantskaya (Commandant's) Tower
(1495, height: 41.25 m)

The tower's original name — Kolyma-zhnaya — came from the Kolymazhny

The hipped roofs of both Komendantskaya and Oruzheinaya towers were built in 1676–1686

Court nearby, which was a garage for royal carriages and carts. The modern name was coined in the 19th century, when the Moscow Commandant moved into the Poteshny Palace next door.

Oruzheinaya (Armory) or Koniushennaya (Stables) Tower
(1495, height: 38.9 m)

The original name — Koniushennaya — derives from the Kremlin Stables, to which the tower's gate provided access in the 17th century. The new name came from the Armory, built nearby in 1851.

Alexandrovsky Garden

The garden, stretching along the Kremlin wall from the Arsenalnaya Angle Tower to the Borovitskie Gate, was arranged concurrently with restoring the Kremlin after the 1812 Franco-Russian War. The Neglinka River, polluted beyond all measure by the locals, was confined inside a pipe. The garden above it was named in honor of Emperor Alexander I, who had defeated Napoleon and liberated Europe from the French occupation. The garden has hardly changed since. The view of the high fortress wall is still as impressive from here as it ever was, especially at sunset. They say the poet Pushkin often came here for inspiration.

Unknown Soldier Memorial

In December 1966, as Russia was celebrating the 25th anniversary of its victory over Nazi troops in the battle of Moscow, the remains

The Unknown Soldier Grave is guarded in shifts by Presidential Regiment soldiers.

of the Unknown Soldier were transferred to the Alexandrovsky Garden from the 41st km of the Leningrad Highway, where the battle took place, and reburied. The Eternal Fire of Glory was lit on the grave, coming out of the center of a bronze star, which is itself positioned in the middle of a black Labrador square, polished to perfection, framed with strips of red granite. The fire was lit from the Eternal Fire at the Revolutionary Fighters Memorial in Mars Field in Leningrad. The Unknown Soldier Grave is guarded in shifts by Presidential Regiment soldiers.

On the right, there is a row of dark-red porphyry slabs along the Kremlin wall, covering urns with the sacred soil of the cities, credited with the "Hero City" title after WWII: Leningrad, Kiev, Minsk, Stalingrad (Volgograd), Sevastopol, Odessa, Kerch, Novorossiysk, Brest Fortress, Tula, Murmansk and Smolensk.

Obelisk
(1913, rebuilt in 1918)

When Russia was celebrating the 300th anniversary of the House of Romanov in 1913, a memorial obelisk was placed in the Alexandrovsky Garden, listing the names of all the Romanovs having ruled Russia over the previous centuries. The Bolsheviks erased the royal names, replacing them with the names of revolutionaries and socialist thinkers.

Grotto Pavilion Ruins
(1820–1823, designed by Osip Bove)

The melancholy grotto ruin stands at the edge of a man-made hill, made for cannons under Peter I's orders when the Czar was expecting the Swedes to attack.

When the grotto was built, there was plenty of material around to build it from as many structures had suffered varying degrees of damage during the brief Napoleonic occupation in 1812. Parts of the partially destroyed Arsenal (which can be seen from here behind the Kremlin wall) also made it into the grotto brickwork. Some of the bricks in the grotto, bearing stamps of various Moscow factories, allow scholars to trace the grotto's history of repairs nearly 200 years back. Perhaps the most unusual part of the brickwork is a rock cannonball 60 cm in diameter. Cannonballs like this were loaded into rock-throwing machines for storming fortresses during the Middle Ages. There is no way of knowing whether the rock was used to attack the Kremlin or defend it.

If you climb the grotto ruin through the vaulted entrance, you can enjoy a scenic view of the Alexandrovsky Garden

Red Square

The area of Red Square is located in the historic confines of the city and is about 4.6 hectares (1 hectare is equivalent to 2.47 acres). It is about 287 m long — from Lobnoe Mesto near the Spasskie Gate to Nikolskie Gate, and about 160 m wide from the Kremlin Wall to the building of Verkhnie Torgovye Riady (now known as GUM).

The best time to enjoy the country's most important square is early morning on a bright day, when the colorful cupolas of St. Basil's Cathedral shine in the sunlight, or at the end of the day, when the ancient towers cast shadows on the cobbles lit bright crimson by the setting sun.

History

The square known today as Red Square originated near Kremlin in 1493. One of great fires destroyed all stalls and barns in Torgovaya (Market) Square, the Kremlin survived only due to its stone walls that had been already built by that time. Then Ivan III took decisive measures and ordered to clear a space of more than 200 m around the walls. Consequently, two squares were formed — Red Square and Manezhnaya (Manege) Square (on the northern side).

In 1508, a defence and fire-prevention ditch was dug along the entire east wall to connect the Neglinny River and the Moskva River having the effect of turning the Kremlin into a medieval Italian fortress. It was built by architect Aloisius the New, therefore the ditch was called Alevizov. Because of the ditch the square was narrower by almost 50 m than it is today. The ditch existed until 1819.

In 1534–1538, during the reign of Ivan the Terrible's mother Elena Glinskaya, Kitai-Gorod (a market district on the eastern side of the Kremlin) was surrounded by a stone wall attached to the Kremlin towers — near Nikolskaya and Uglovaya Arsenalnaya in the north and Moskvoretskaya in the south. As a result, Red Square became part of a large confined space. In the 18th–19th centuries all sections of the Kitai-Gorod wall near the square were gradually dismantled.

In the 16th century, there was a square located near the Alevizov ditch taking its name from the Church of the Holy Trinity. In 1561 it was substituted by the St. Basil's Cathedral but the square retained its former name for some time.

Despite numerous laws prohibiting constructions, unauthorized structures were put there quite often. The stalls caught fire so often that the place got the name Pozhar (meaning "fire" in Russian).

The look of Red Square nowdays

By the late 17th century the square was known as "Red", derived from the Old Slavonic, meaning "beautiful". Officially this name was not registered until the 19th century. The market moved from the square to the east, to Kitai-Gorod.

At that time a tavern called "Under the Cannons" was a very popular place. It was located near the Nikolskaya Tower under a stone platform about 3 m tall with cannons on top of it. The platform was erected in the time of Czar Mikhail in the 1610s to protect the Nikolskie Gate but was never used for this purpose. In the late 17th century the land was leased to a merchant, Danilov, who opened a tavern there. He polished the cannons on the roof until they shined and even built a fence around the Cathedral of Our Lady of Kazan at his own expense. The tavern outlasted a dozen of czars, emperors and empresses, and was shut down only in the second half of the 18th century.

Fireworks in Red Square celebrated the change of calendar from the traditional Russian calendar to the Western one from

← **The monument to Minin and Pozharsky, the first monument in Moscow, was originally placed in the center of Red Square opposite the main entrance to the Verkhnie Torgogye Ryady**

1 January 1700 by Decree of Peter the Great. In 1722, to commemorate victory in the Northern War a triumphal arch was erected in the square following the same design as the triumphal arches of Ancient Rome. A procession of an entire flotilla on wheels under sail passed through the arch from the Voskresenskie Gate to the Kremlin for a formal reception accompanied by ringing of the bells and cannonades.

Not long before Napoleon's invasion in 1804 the square was paved with cobbles. In 1812, Napoleon drew up

Napoleon looks on as fire glows over the Kremlin in 1812

his troops there to congratulate them with the seizure of Moscow. The French were accommodated in the St. Basil's Cathedral, which they used as the stables. After the fire and the flight of the French from Moscow, semi-destroyed buildings in Red Square were demolished.

In 1892 the square was electrified. It had previously been lit by oil lamps put on high poles.

In the early 20th century after long disputes between the City Administration and the Moscow Archeological Society, tram tracks were built across the square.

In the 1930s, the square underwent large reconstruction: the Voskresenskie Gate with the Iverskaya Chapel was dismantled; the Cathedral of Our Lady of Kazan was demolished; the tram tracks were taken off; the cobblestone pavement was substituted by stoneblocks; the monument to Minin and Pozharsky, which used to stand in the center of the square, was moved to its current location before St. Basil's Cathedral. All this was done to make way for the May Day processions and military vehicles during the military parades of the October Revolution celebrations.

In the 1990s, the Cathedral of Our Lady of Kazan and the Voskresenskie Gate with the Iverskaya Chapel were reconstructed. It is through the Voskresenskie Gate that people usually proceed to Red Square but before we go there, we will stop to discuss the buildings nearby.

Over the centuries Red Square has been reconstructed many times. Red Square in the 17th century

The Building of the Former Provincial Administration

At the very entrance to Red Square, on the left of the Voskresenskie Gate, there is an old building which was constructed in the time of Empress Anna (architect Ivan Geiden) in the early Baroque style and later belonged to the Provincial Administration.

In the courtyard, which is unfortunately inaccessible, the remains of the first Russian mint can be found. The mint was established during the reign of Peter I in 1697. Later the basement of the former state treasury accommodated the debtor's prisons, which made some sense. The prison was more known as "the Pit". Debtors, mostly merchants, were kept there until they paid off their debts. The prison was literally a pit — it was a small rectangular courtyard 7 meters deep with warm "residential" quarters around it. Access to the courtyard from the square was unimpeded, and until a guard was put at the entrance crowds of gapers gathered there.

The living conditions in the Pit were quite tolerable. There were separate chambers for nobles, merchants and the low middle class and even a chamber for women as well as a churchmen, a kitchen and a bathhouse. There was a custom according to which Moscow merchants sent to the Pit baskets full of home-baked rolls, ham, liqueurs, etc. on important Russian Orthodox holidays. It is interesting to note that the creditors covered all the expenses of keeping debtors in prison, and the stop of financing meant that the prisoner was released. It is not quite understandable why the Pit was called "a dreadful place for a merchant" in the pre-Revolutionary guidebooks.

The State Historic Museum

The building of the State Historic Museum on the right of the Voskresenskie Gate was built in 1875–1881 (architect Valisly Shervud and engineer Alexander Semenov). It houses about 4.5 million exhibits and more than 15 million pages of documents. About 22 thousands exhibits are on display. If one walked three kilometers through its rooms and spent a minute at each exhibit, it would take 360 hours. Today it is one of the largest collections of Russian history in the world and is worth a visit.

From 1700 on this site there was a building of the Land Office (a central governmental agency regulating Moscow, taxation, and law cases) featuring 3 floors and a turret topped with a double eagle. Unlike the building of the museum it was not particularly significant neither in terms of exterior nor interior but nevertheless went down to history. Firstly, it accommodated the first pharmacy in Russia. Secondly, it accommodated the first Chinese restaurant in Russia. And finally, it accommodated the

The view of Red Square in the first half of the 19th century

famous Moscow University founded by Mikhail Lomonosov in 1755.

The Voskresenskie Gate with the Iverskaya Chapel

The gate with the chapel demolished in 1929–1931 was reconstructed in 1995 to have the look they used to have in the reign of Feodor in the 17th century. Due to the miracle-making Iverskaya icon of the Mother of God this gate was more often called Iverskie or the Holy Gate.

According to the old custom, emperors and empresses stopped at the Voskresenskie Gate upon entering Moscow to pray in the chapel before proceeding to the Kremlin. Common pilgrims stopped to kneel before the Iverskaya icon when coming to the center of the ancient capital. Nowadays all visitors to Moscow also stop at this place which mark the so-called "zero" kilometer of Russia.

Iverskie Gate is part of the wall (to put it more precisely, reconstructed) which used to go around Kitai-Gorod from the Nikolskie Gate. The height and the length of the gate is approximately the same (25.5 m and 24 m, respectively), the width being about 8.5 m.

According to legend, the barred windows with dark mica were put in at the request of Moscow queens and princesses so that they could watch the ceremonial processions and foreign ambassadors entering the Kremlin. The white niches in the wall right above the gate ("gutters") were designed for pouring melted tar and boiled water on the heads of enemies. Fortunately, they were never used for this purpose.

In olden times there was only a small passage in the wall of Kitai-Gorod. In the time of Czar Alexius in the 17th century a wider gate was built which became the main gate. So many heavy-loaded carts entered Kitai-Gorod that soon the gate fell totally into decay. In 1680 Czar Feodor gave orders for the gate to be split into two parts and for arches to be built in order to preserve the property. In the middle between the arches a

A sculpure of an angel holding a cross is believed to be installed on the roof of the Chapel at the suggestion of Alexander I

chapel was built described as "a wooden chapel with a closet" — this building remained a wooden structure until the middle of the 18th century.

The Iverskaya Chapel was the most famous in old Moscow, but despite this fact it was demolished in 1722 by order of the Holy Synod adopted under pressure from Peter the Great along with other chapels in the city. However, it was soon reconstructed in 1727 after the Emperor's death.

During the Great Fire of 1737 in the reign of Empress Anna the gate as well as the chapel burned down. The Iverskaya icon was saved while the other ones perished in the fire. After the coronation of Catherine II in 1762 a new tradition appeared — to decorate this gate for ceremonial entries to the Kremlin, and it received another name — the Triumphal Gate. In 1756 Russia's first civic printing-house attached to the Moscow University was accommodated in the Gate.

The look of Voskresenskie (Resurrection) Gate with Iverskaya Chapel in the 21st century

The Cathedral of Our Lady of Kazan

The Cathedral of Our Lady of Kazan is to the left of the passage through the Voskresenskie Gate, and was rebuilt to its present form and consecrated in 1993. Today it is

More than three centuries later the Cathedral of Our Lady of Kazan looks almost the same as it used to in the 17th century

the only church in the historic area of the Kremlin and Red Square where services are conducted on a regular basis. Now we can see the Cathedral as it was designed and built in the 17th century. Its elegant and festive look as well as its location emphasizes the memorial meaning of the church. It was constructed originally to commemorate the great victory of the Russian people over the Polish invaders, which put an end to numerous hardships in the Time of Troubles. The home guards who liberated Moscow vowed to built it.

In the second half of the 17th century the church became known as the stronghold of the dissenters who opposed the reforms of Patriarch Nikon and continued to practice the old rituals. It was to the Cathedral of Our Lady of Kazan that Nikon sent his first charter ordering them to adopt crossing themselves with three fingers instead of two and to bow instead of kneeling. However, Archpriest Ivan Neronov refused to obey the Patriarch's order and gave shelter to Archdeacon Avvakum, the leader of old believers.

From the porch of the church in the immediate vicinity of the Kremlin that the old believers gathered and preached opposition to the Patriarch. Avvakum and approximately 60 parishioners were arrested in the middle of an all-night service. The rebellious archdeacon was exiled to Siberia and after 15-year imprisonment in earth prison ended his life at the stake.

Over several centuries of its existence the Cathedral of Our Lady of Kazan was been rebuilt many times. In 1865, it was totally rebuilt. In the 1920s it was restored to the design and appearance that it had in the 17th century but in 1936, 300 years after of its foundation, it was demolished. The new church was erected on the old foundation of the 17th century found during excavations.

The Icon of Our Lady of Kazan

One of the most worshiped icons in Russia, the icon that helped to liberate Moscow in 1612, used to be located in the icon stand on the left of the Holy Doors. Now you can see one of its replicas (19th century).

The Icon of Our Lady of Kazan had been acquired in 1579, almost 30 years after Ivan the Terrible conquered Kazan. According to a legend, a nine-year-old girl who lived in the new Kazan Eparchy saw in her dream the Mother of God who came to her three times and asked to remove the icon which was hidden underground. The icon of the

The miracle-making Icon of our Lady of Kazan that used to belong to Prince Pozharsky is now in the Theophany Cathedral in Moscow. Since time immemorial the Icon of Our Lady of Kazan was worshiped as the healer of eye diseases

Mother of Christ was found wrapped in a piece of cloth. To everyone's surprise, the icon was brand new as if just painted. It is still unknown who buried it or when. Since then 8 (21) July has been a festive day, celebrating the icon's acquisition.

Until the end of the 17th century twice a year on holy days the icon was carried around on the walls of the Kremlin and Kitai-Gorod, and Russian czars as well as the Patriarch participated in these processions. A procession with the relics from the Cathedral of the Assumption and other Kremlin churches went to Red Square through the Spasskie Gate. Processions from all the churches in Moscow, bearing their relics also came there. In Lobnoe Mesto, the Patriarch crossed Moscow with the Icon of Our Lady of Kazan, and the processions withdrew to different parts of the city. One of them, lead by an archdeacon, climbed the walls of the Kremlin and went around it.

One of the replicas of the icon became the main relic of the home guards formed and headed by K. Minin and D. Pozharsky to liberate the country from the Polish-Lithuanian invaders in the 17th century.

When the home guards approached Moscow, Pozharsky saw a terrible picture. The local armed groups were fighting with each other, the Cossacks and other mercenaries were plundering the civilian population. The Poles were blocked up in the fortress in the middle of a foreign country, and though worn out by hunger showed strong resistance, and the Russians were unable to dislodge them from the Kremlin for a long time. Then a thanksgiving service was held before the Icon of Our Lady of Kazan. For three days the home guards fasted and prayed and then they started their attack. On 22 October (4 November of the Gregorian calendar), Kitai-Gorod was taken, and three days later the troops headed by Pozharsky entered the Kremlin. These events are commemorated by the second annual celebration of the miracle-making icon (established in 1613), and since 2005 the day of 4 November has been celebrated as a new state holiday — the Day of National Unity.

On 21 February 1613, the Land Assembly ruled that a the Romanov-Yurievy dynasty who were related to the former Rurikid dynasty would ascend the throne. Since then the Kazan Icon had become the second family relic of the Romanov Dynasty. The Feodorovskaya Icon of Our Lady from the Ipatievsky Monastery in Kostroma is considered to be the first one.

The icon that used to belong to the Pozharsky's home guards was put in the Cathedral of Our Lady of Kazan. In 1721, when the capital was moved to St. Petersburg, Peter the Great also moved there the miracle-

Prince Pozharsky before the Icon of Our Lady of Kazan receiving a blessing for the struggle with the invaders

making Kazan Icon — the protector of the royal dynasty — which used to stand in the Cathedral of the Assumption in the Kremlin. The Cathedral of Our Lady of Kazan, much more magnificent than the Moscow church was built in St. Petersburg and dedicated to the Icon. Since then the icon of Prince Pozharsky has become the main icon of Our Lady of Kazan in Moscow. All three icons (in Kazan, Moscow, and St. Petersburg) were worshiped as for their miracles. The icon that remained in Kazan was stolen in 1904. Many believe that it was the icon that was kept in Vatican for a long time and returned to the Russian Orthodox Church in 2004.

The Mausoleum and the Necropolis
Mausoleum is a memorial burial-vault where a crystal sarcophagus with the body of V. I. Lenin lies in the Hall of Mourning. It was built in 1930 to the plans of architect Alexius Schusev and substituted the tempo-

Behind the Mausoleum are the graves of Soviet rulers, each with a bust on its tombstone

rary wooden mausoleum erected in January of 1924. At the same time on both sides of the building guest rostrums were built to accommodate 10,000 people.

Back in 1917 in the territory behind the present mausoleum a necropolis was founded –more than 200 revolutionaries who perished fighting for the Soviet government were buried there. In later years prominent bolsheviks were buried in the necropolis, and over 100 urns with the ashes of outstanding Soviet statesmen, heads of the international communist and labor movement, scientists, writers, prominent military leaders, pilots, astronauts and other heroes of the Soviet era were placed inside the Kremlin wall. 12 statesmen of the Soviet Union, including all leaders except Nikita Khruschev (who is buried at Novodevichie

Cemetery), were buried in individual tombs: Yakov Sverdlov, Mikhail Frunze, Felix Dzerzhinsky, Mikhail Kalinin, Andrei Zhdanov, Josef Stalin, Kliment Voroshilov, Semen Budenny, Mikhail Suslov, Leonid Brezhnev, Yury Andropov, and Konstantin Chernenko. It should be noted that the body of Josef Stalin after his death in 1953 was embalmed and lay in the mausoleum along with the body of V. I. Lenin until 1961. At that time the situation in the USSR changed: Josef Stalin was found guilty of political purges, and the body of the former mighty dictator was committed to the earth.

GUM
The eastern side of the square is occupied by the buildings of GUM, which is the abbreviation for the Main Universal Store in Russian. In Soviet times the "G" stood for "State". Some time ago this shopping mall was one of the largest in Europe.

From the time the Kremlin was being constructed there had been a large market or Torg nearby, providing a source of income for the Kremlin. Various duties imposed on merchants were used to finance the construction of churches and fortifications.

Peter the Great who badly needed money for the war with Sweden and the

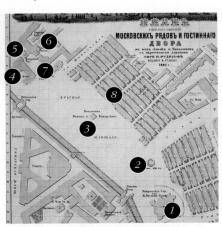

Legend to the plan of Red Square dated 1861
1. **Pokrovsky Sobor (St. Basil's Cathedral)**
2. **Lobnoe Mesto**
3. **Monument to Minin and Pozharsky is now nearby Pokrovsky sobor**
4. **The former Land Office, now the State Historic Museum**
5. **The Voskresenskie Gate with the Iverskaya Chapel**
6. **"The Pit" – debtor's prison**
7. **The Cathedral of Our Lady of Kazan**
8. **Upper Shopping Rows, now GUM**

construction of St. Petersburg invented an additional way of replenishing the coffers. He established a post at the Spasskie (Savoir) Gate and fined people who refused to shave their beards in the European fashion. Many pilgrims had first to go to the nearest barber in Kitai-Gorod before entering the Kremlin.

Until the 15th century the main market was located right in the vicinity where Red Square now lies. After Ivan III had cleared this

The image of the Savior reappeared in the stone icon case on the building of GUM (former Verkhnie Torgovye Raydy) in the1990s.

space, the stores moved to the east and filled up all nearby blocks. Thus torgovye ryady or "shopping rows" were formed. They got the name "Verkhnie" (Upper) because they were located on elevated territory. Only small stalls remained in Red Square.

The Rows were named by the goods and services they traded in: Ikonny (icons), Lapotny (bast shoes), Nozhenoi (knives), Nitny (threads), Zhemchuzhny (pearls), Sedelny (saddles), Zhelezny (hardware),

Maslyany (oils and butter), Vetchinny (ham), Ovoschnoi (vegetables), Kruzhevnoi (lace), and Serebryany (silver). In the Obzhorny Ryad (Glutton Row) one could relish a delicious ukha (fish soup) and sbiten (a hot honey drink). In the Vshivy Ryad (Lice Row) one could use the services of barbers and hairdressers.

In the late 16th century the first masonry Verkhnie Torgovye Ryady (Upper Shopping Rows) were built, and in 17th century almost all retail and wholesale trade in Moscow was concentrated there.

After Napoleon's invasion and the fire of 1812, architect Osip Bove was commissioned with the reconstruction of Red Square and he erected a new building for Verkhnie Torgovye Ryady in the Empire style. However it served solely to screen off the cramped mazes of the market.

In the late 19th century the merchants set up a joint-stock company and raised a large amount of capital to finance construction of a new building. Architect Alexander Pomerantsev, who suggested a grandiose building in the Neo-Russian style with three passages under one glass roof, won the competition to construct a new building. This roof was designed by an engineer V. Shukhov who was also the designer of the famous radio and television tower in Shabolovka Street in Moscow.

Even at that time the new shopping galleries tended to be universal and in addition to selling goods provided services of porters, barbers, postmen, bankers and even dentists. Since then the notion of being universal has expanded significantly, which one can see by taking a walk inside this impressive store.

Lobnoe Mesto

Opposite Spasskie Gate there is Lobnoe Mesto — a high platform behind the cast-iron lattice, which appeared here in the middle of the 16th century. The round rostrum is made of natural ashlar and faced with white stone, which symbolizes both its role in the square and also the stone which was placed over the grave of the Savoir and rolled aside following his resurrection.

Pre-Revolutionary share of Verkhnie Torgovye Ryady. In the post-Soviet time GUM also became a joint-stock company

This look Lobnoe Mesto had in the 19th century

Unlike similar platforms in the squares of Ancient Greece and Rome, this place was not for a tribune of the people. The parapet was always latticed although formerly the lattice was wooden.

Lobnoe Mesto was used for special occasions such as for reading the decrees of the czars, displaying the relics intended for the Kremlin churches or announcing a death sentences on state criminals. Czars came out here when necessary to pacify the people or secure their support. Sometimes it was used to publicly recant, as Ivan the Terrible did, or to make a speech in celebration of the New Year, as Czar Alexius did. In the 16th–17th centuries, preaching and reading of the Gospel was conducted here during the church services since the St. Basil's Cathedral was too cramped.

Lobnoe Mesto is associated with numerous myths and legends. However, contrary to a common belief, executions never took place in Lobnoe Mesto. Scaffolds were put near it and more often in Vasilievsky Spusk behind St. Basil's Cathedral. For executions, special gibbets or gallows were made from wood. They were burned after the sentence was carried out, after which the place was consecrated during a special service.

In Orthodox Moscow, this place also symbolized Calvary of Jerusalem (or Golgotha) where Jesus Christ was crucified. The Gospel according to Mathew says: "and when they were come unto a place called Golgotha, that is to say, "a place of a skull" (Mt 27, 33). In the Gospel according to Luke it is said: "and when they were come to the place, which is called Calvary, there they crucified him" (Lk 23, 33). According to a religious belief, under this mountain there is Adam's skull (or "forehead" which is "lob" in Russian) that was washed with Jesus Christ's blood. Therefore an elevation with steps in front of the Kremlin was also called "lobnoe". Along with the St. Basil's Cathedral and the Spasskie Gate, Lobnoe Mesto was part of a gigantic open air church. It also symbolized the center of the land, like special structures in Rome and Constantinople. There is an ancient map of Russia on which all distances were taken from this place.

Lobnoe Mesto was first mentioned in the chronicles under its actual name in 1549 when the first convention of representatives of all classes — the Land Assembly — took place in Moscow.

The main issue under discussion was abuse of power by local boyars who in the name of the czar levied unauthorized taxes on cities and volosts (districts), which brought the country to decay. The 20-year-old Czar Ivan the Terrible mounted Lobnoe Mesto and said that he did not know anything about such unruliness because of his young age and asked the offended to

Lobnoe Mesto often became the scene of significant historical events

forgive the boyars in a Christian way. He told the boyars to become reconciled with the taxpayers and not to rob them in the future. Evidently, the czar was a talented orator despite his young age because, according to the author of The Stepennaya Book, the astounded people burst into tears and the hostile parties started hugging one another.

Here in 1613 the people unanimously expressed their will when young Mikhail Romanov was elected czar. According to the chronicler, when the news was announced, the crowd shouted: "Let Mikhail be the ruler over all Muscovy!"

When the Time of Troubles ended, a tradition appeared in Moscow that confused foreigners. When a heir to the throne turned 16 years of age, he was taken to Lobnoe Mesto and introduced to people. It was done in order to make people remember their future legitimate czar and not to let imposters ascend the Russian throne. Before that he was not allowed to deal with anyone except his nearest circle.

A German traveler Adam Olearius who visited Moscow in the middle of the 17th century called Lobnoe Mesto "the theatre of proclamations" (meaning the place for orators' speeches). Czar Alexius had to mount this platform several times during his challenging reign (marked with plague, bad harvests, riots, uprisings, inflation and

Pussy-willow market in Red Square

religious dissent) in order to pacify people "with kind and endearing words".

Pious and sensitive Czar Alexius also liked participating in another ritual — a famous "procession on a donkey" on a Palm Sunday. The splendid procession reproduced the entry of Jesus Christ into Jerusalem. The Patriarch played the role of the Savior. He mounted Lobnoe Mesto, blessed the congregation and gave out consecrated pussy-willow and palm branches that were

In the 17th century "the procession on the donkey" was performed — an evangelic event of Jesus Christ's entry into Jerusalem. The Partriarch himself played the role the Lord

specially brought from the Orient to the Czar and his confidants. Then the Patriarch mounted a white horse fitted out like a donkey and proceeded to the Kremlin as if it was Jerusalem. Czar Alexius lead the horse holding the bridle-reigns with a humble look demonstrating to all people in Moscow that Nikon's words "Priesthood is higher than czardom" were correct.

In September-October 1698, Peter the Great suppressed the mutiny of the Strelets guards who constituted the czar's troops and whom the former regent Sophia was trying to use in her struggle for power. The Strelets guards, who had confessed to high treason, were gathered at Lobnoe Mesto. They came in with dropped heads in regular ranks. Each detachment was carrying a scaffold and axes for cutting their heads off. Hundreds of Strelets guards were hung on the Kremlin walls and in Vasilievsky Spusk.

For the number of those who were executed by Lobnoe Mesto Peter the Great was almost equal to Ivan he Terrible. After the capital was moved to St. Petersburg, the carnage in Red Square stopped.

The "golden age" of Catherine II began with a bonfire. On 4 June 1763, a manifesto with a long title "On Prohibiting Indecent Discussions and Speculations about Affairs Related to the Government" was announced from Lobnoe Mesto, and accompanied by

Nowadays Red Square does not resound with czars' decrees or calls of miserable tramps begging for some change or the death-throes of executed criminals. It has become the major scene of events during public and big religious holidays

the beat of the drums indecent books, in which Empress was criticized for her German descent as well as the St. Petersburg elite, were burned. Later so-called "pillories" were put by Lobnoe Mesto to expose the convicted to public condemnation since capital punishment in Russia was banned by Empress Elizabeth in 1743.

In 1768 a landowner Daria Saltykova was put in the pillory for torturing 139 of her serfs to death. She wore a shroud and held a candle that is usually given to a dead person, which meant that there was no place for her in this world.

The painting "The Morning of the Strelets Guards Execution" by Vasily Surikov depicts the moment directly before the execution. A young Peter the Great (a horseman on a white horse) meets the eyes of an unrepentant mutineer. Neither strelets guards brought for the execution, nor their wives or children ask for forgiveness. In a few minutes the irrevocable will occur

In the late 18th century it was intended to punish here a noble man called Istomin for forgery of serf-ownership deeds. After reading the decree, the executor forced him to his knees, broke the sword over his head, and slapped him in the face. The insulted noble-man sprang to his feet and delivered such a blow in return that the executor fell over the fence of the scaffold on the ground. The public burst out laughing, and there were no more civil executions in Red Square afterwards.

In August 1914, the Emperor's Manifesto declaring war on Germany was read from Lobnoe Mesto as well as in other public venues of Moscow.

The Bolsheviks intended to use Lobnoe Mesto for propaganda. On 1 May 1919 a monument to Stepan Razin was made hastily from planks covered with gypsum and painted. Lenin mounted the platform and delivered a fiery speech about "a representative of mutinous peasants who gave his life at this place struggling for freedom". However, the leaders did not attempt to make speeches with the St. Basil's Cathedral at the background any more. Soon they built their own memorial by the Kremlin wall and their own platform, which totally changed the look and the character of Red Square.

Around Spasskie Gate

In the area between the Spassky Bridge and the St. Basil's Cathedral for almost 150 years from the late 16th century until 1722 there was Popovsky Krestets — a place where residents of Moscow could hire a priest or a deacon who were not assigned to any particular church to serve a liturgy or any other occasional rites at home. As many houses used to have home churches, such services were in great demand.

The people who had home churches, which were usually quite affluent, came here

Sale stores nearby the Spassky Bridge in the 18th century

early in the morning and bargained desperately. Having agreed on the price, they went to a nearby building by the Kremlin wall where the Patriarch's office was located (so-called Tiunskaya Izba) and paid a duty to the Patriarch's coffer from the agreed amount.

The area around the St. Basil's Cathedral was occupied by the beggars and the saintly simpletons (yurodivys) who worshiped St. Basil and St. John of Moscow. Before the reign of Peter the Great, there were about fifty of them. There was a strict hierarchy among the beggars, each was allocated a small area, and outsiders were not allowed in. In 1703 by his decree Peter the Great banned begging in Moscow thus putting an end to this trade.

Monument to Minin and Pozharsky

A bronze monument depicts one of the dramatic episodes of the Russian history. Prince Dmitry Pozharsky wounded in the course of an unsuccessful battle is looking into the distance leaning against a shield with the image of the Savior — he had prayed before this image in the Spaso-Evfimievsky Monastery before setting off on the campaign. The athletically built merchant Kuzma Minin-Sukhoruk is handing him a sword and asking to protect the independence of Russia and banish the enemy from the homeland. The Russian patriots are depicted as antique heroes but the elements of national clothing intentionally make Minin look like a common peasant.

Book stores by the Spassky Bridge in the 16th century

The Monument to Minin and Pozharsky

son also enlisted as a volunteer during the Patriotic War of 1812. The back bas-relief depicts a romanticized scene of banishing the Poles from Moscow.

A gilded inscription on the pedestal says: "To citizen Minin and Prince Pozharsky from grateful Russia".

Originally the monument was located in the center of Red Square opposite the main entrance to the Verkhnie Torgovye Ryady (GUM). Minin pointed his arm towards the Kremlin urging his comrade to liberate Moscow. Now, after moving the monument in 1931, the two national heroes stand behind the fence of the St. Basil's Cathedral, and the meaning of the gesture has been lost.

Vasilievsky Spusk

In the square behind St. Basil's Cathedral near the Moscow River, in the 16th–17th centuries there was a "customs station". The cattle, hogs, and poultry entering Moscow passed through it. For each head a certain duty was paid to the government and a stamp was put on the animal without which the sale of animals or poultry was prohibited in Moscow.

Many different wooden buildings used to be put in the area around St. Basil's Cathedral which added little to its beauty. From time to time they were demolished either after fires or in an attempt to improve the territory. In the reign of Alexander I Vasilievskaya Square was built behind the Cathedral with a smooth descent to the Moscow River (now the square is called Vasilivsky Spusk).

On both sides of the polished granite pedestal there are bas-reliefs. The facade bas-relief depicts citizens of Nizhny Novgorod who donate their savings and set up a militia to liberate Moscow. The last figure on the left, a father, who is sending his sons to war, is the author of the monument Ivan Petrovich Martos, Rector of the Academy of Fine Arts in St. Petersburg. His

Pokrovsky Sobor
(Cathedral of the Intercession
of the Virgin on the Moat)

The Cathedral of the Intercession with its unusual combination of domes, artful forms and overall harmony is a superb, unmatched masterpiece of Russian architecture, and probably the most celebrated and mysterious temple in Russia. Its real name is the Cathedral of the Intercession of the Holy Virgin, Which is on the Moat (the Aloisius Moat, running along the Kremlin wall nearby, was filled in the early 1800s), but the temple is better known as the Cathedral of St. Basil the Blessed, or St. Basil's. The central ribbed roof is surrounded by eight onions, none of them the same as the others, signifying eight Chapeles, each dedicated to its own saint or event, connected by galleries.

In contrast to its fascinating exterior, the cathedral is disappointingly small inside. There is not enough room for many people to pray at the same time. The cramped rooms, low gallery vaults and narrow passageways seem more appropriate for a Medieval home, not a place of worship. We can assume that the cathedral was originally intended to impress with its exterior appearance only.

History

St. Basil's Cathedral was built in 1555–1561 under orders from Ivan the Terrible with the blessing of Metropolitan Macarius in honor of the Russian conquest of Kazan and the Kazan Khanate in 1552. The full and final defeat of Tartar troops on their home turf was an inspiration to all Russian people.

← **At first glance, the church may seem to be devoid of any symmetry whatsoever, but the symmetry will reveal itself if you look at it from outside the western annex, dedicated to the Entry of Our Lord into Jerusalem.**

Engraving from the book by Adam Olearius, based on a drawing from the 1630s

The Battle of Kazan was compared to the Battle of Kulikovo Polye, which had ended centuries of Tartar Mongolian rule in Russia. Upon his return from Kazan, the Czar threw a sumptuous feast in the Kremlin that went on for several days with lavish gifts for everyone.

The original wooden Cathedral of the Intercession of the Holy Virgin with seven Chapeles was consecrated on 1 October 1554. Some of the Chapeles were dedicated to the saints whose holidays had coincided with Kazan campaign highlights: August 30 (according to the old calendar), when the Russians had defeated a large Tartar troop led by Prince Epancha; is the day of three Constantinople Patriarchs: Alexander, John and Paul, as well as St. Alexander of Svir. On September 30, the day dedicated to Gregory, the enlightener of Armenia, the Russians had captured a part of the Kazan fortress wall and the Arsk tower. Kazan was stormed and conquered on October 2, Sts. Cyprian and Justina Day. These dedication and the choice of location for the new temple continued a tradition started by Vasily III, Ivan the Terrible's father, who had ordered a Cathedral built by the moat to commemorate his conquest of Smolensk, dedicating its altars to the saints whose name days coincided with the day of his victory over Smolensk. The older church had burned down during one of Moscow's many fires.

Another altar in the new Cathedral was consecrated in honor of St. Varlaam of Khutyn, possibly in memory of Vasily III who had, at the end of his life, taken monastic vows as was the custom for Russian rulers at the time. Basil's monastic name was Varlaam. The altar in the easterly Chapel

Pokrovsky Sobor

was dedicated to the Holy Trinity, while the main altar was dedicated to the Holy Virgin's patronage over all Christians. Virgin Mary is specially worshipped in the Russian Orthodox tradition as a celestial protector. On Intercession of the Holy Virgin Day, Kazan had stood besieged, and soon fell. The westerly Chapel was dedicated to the Entry of Jesus into Jerusalem. This holiday was marked with a "donkey procession" (described in the Red Square chapter). Before the Cathedral of the Intercession was built, the procession had always stayed inside the Kremlin walls. It is possible that the Czar had had a change of the procession itinerary in mind when he ordered the Cathedral built. From then on, the procession would walk from the Kremlin to the new temple.

Ivan the Terrible soon ordered the Cathedral rebuilt in stone. According to historical evidence, the architects "Barma and Postnik Yakovlev," hired to design the stone Cathedral, had originally designed it with nine altars, and here is why.

Soon before the construction began, the Czar had received visitors from the town of Khlynov (Viatka), bringing the tidings of a new miracle-working icon of St. Nicholas Velikoretsky. The icon had survived a devastating church fire with only minor damage, and the envoys from Viatka were seeking the Czar's permission to bring it to Moscow for restoration. The Czar had prayed to St. Nicholas repeatedly during his Kazan campaign, so the appearance of a new miraculous St. Nicholas icon was conceived as the saint's blessing for what the Czar had done, instituting Orthodox Christianity in the Kazan lands and annexing them to Muscovy. Ivan the Terrible ordered the icon delivered to Moscow immediately, and decided to dedicate the ninth Chapel of his new Cathedral to St. Nicholas. The icon was shipped by riverboat across the Kazan lands as a semblance of the Procession of the Cross

Chalice donated by Czar Mikhail. The inscription on the top rim is a quote from a prayer: "Drink of this..."

Icon of St Nicholas of Velikoretskoe, 16th century

across the previously pagan Tartar Khanate, now conquered by Russia.

When the Cathedral was completed, it was painted in the brickwork pattern. In actual fact, the temple was built in brick in the first place; only its foundation, basement, and some decorations were made in white stone. A standalone bell tower was built at the Cathedral's southeastern corner at around the same time.

In 1588, during the reign of Feodor, another church was built here on the grave of Basil the Blessed, a street prophet worshipped in Moscow at the time, who had died in 1557. Unlike the other Chapels of the Cathedral of the Intercession, this church held daily sermons, so it wasn't long before parishioners started calling the whole cathedral St. Basil's.

Churches in Red Square, early 1600s

The cathedral underwent some major remodeling at the end of the 17th century: the outdoor wraparound gallery was covered with vaults; ribbed awnings were built over the entrances, and a northerly Chapel was added to the Basil the Blessed Church as a second level, dedicated to Theodosia the Virgin. Soon another church was built next to St. Basil's, dedicated to another worshipped "God's Fool," named John but better known under the nickname "Big Fool's Cap," buried here in 1589. More remodeling was done to make room for the altars of several other churches that had stood in Red Square, but were pulled down due to disrepair. The floral ornaments on the vestibules and porches were painted around the same time.

Many of the "guest" altars were "retired" during the reign of Catherine II in the 18th century, and the Cathedral was repainted according to the artistic fashion of the epoch.

The cathedral acquired its present colorful look after a succession of restorations in the 20th century, which restored the temple to its 16th–17th century look. The motley onion domes were painted the way they were in the 19th century.

We will just mention one of the many legends that surround St. Basil's Church. It is claimed that Ivan the Terrible ordered the architects of St. Basil's blinded so that they never build an amazing temple like this again. In fact, similar legends exist in many cultures about their own treasured masterpieces. Our only source on this is the travelogue of a German traveler named Adam Olearius who visited Moscow in the 17th century. No Russian chroniclers ever mentioned the blinding.

Icon of St. Basil the Beatific

Holy Relics at St. Basil's

A Moscow street prophet, Basil the Blessed, was buried by the Cathedral's northeastern wall in 1557. According to legend, Basil was revered and feared by Ivan the Terrible himself as a Holy Fool (Yourodivy).

Such person was someone who had voluntarily rejected earthly comforts and pleasures. Under the guise of insanity, these people defied all shame and decency. (Usually, these "God's Fools" were quite sane, sensible — or at least extremely brave — people). A beatific person would affront and offend other people by wallowing in the mud, walking around naked, and shouting insults. At the same time, God's Fools were under the special unspoken patronage of the Church. Like Basil, many of them were posthumously canonized as saints. Like court jesters, yurodivye freaks were "entitled" to say things to the rulers for which a regular person would face immediate punishment by death.

Originally, Basil the Blessed had had nothing to do with the Cathedral. He was simply buried here while the temple was still under construction, and later another church was built on the grave, adjacent to the Cathedral. But today most people apply the name St. Basil's to the whole temple, and have no idea that the Cathedral actually has a different name.

St. Basil was born in 1469 in Elokhovo near Moscow, and was trained to be a shoemaker. Basil displayed his prophetic gift quite early. He became a yurodivyi at age 16, leading an ascetic life and teaching people about religion and morality. Basil lived a very long life. The 1588 Church Assembly canonized Basil as a saint, while Czar Feodor

Pokrovsky Sobor

Façade Icon of the Sign of the Holy Virgin on the easterly cathedral wall was worshipped and believed to work miracles, particularly in matters of conception and childbirth

ordered a silver gold-plated shrine encrusted with gems and pearls erected above the grave of a man who had never worn any clothes and had begged for food all his life.

In the southeasterly wing of the Cathedral, which is closed to general public, the relics of another yurodivyi lie under a bushel. St. John, nicknamed "Big Fool's Cap," died in 1589. John walked around barefoot all year, wearing nothing but a cloak with a large hood (hence his nickname). John wore long hair, a heavy copper cross on his chest, fetters, copper rings on his fingers, and an iron cap. He would publicly expose the sins of Boris Godunov before the latter became Czar, and predicted Godunov's bitter end. John was canonized in 1672. Originally, a precious silver-plated shrine stood on his grave on which lay his fetters, weighing around 40 kg, and his iron cap. The shrine was requisitioned following the 1917 Bolshevik coup, but the fetters and the cap are on display in the Cathedral museum.

The fresco icon The Sign of God's Mother, sized 2.84 by 2.84 m, was painted specially for the cathedral in the early 18th century. The icon, placed outside on the easterly wall of the Holy Trinity Chapel, was worshipped and considered miraculous.

A modified copy on wood was made of this icon in the 1780s, with a slightly different lineup of saints at the edges. This copy used to hang above the entrance to the St. Basil the Blessed Church. It is now on display on the ground floor.

Another large façade icon, The Intercession of Our Lady, sized 2.6 by 3.8 m, was painted in the 1780s. It is now on the southerly wall of the Cathedral belfry.

Chapels of St. Basil's

One architectural peculiarity of St. Basil's is that it consists of nine individual Chapels sharing a foundation. Four tall pillar-like Chapels are centered around the main Chapel, facing east, west, north and south, with four lower Chapels in between.

The cathedral has two roofed porches, but the only functioning entry for visitors is through St. Basil's Church. Its existing iconostasis and murals date back to the late 19th – early 20th centuries. The precious shrine over St. Basil's grave was looted by Polish soldiers during the Time of Troubles period; the existing shrine was made in 1896, displaying scenes from the saint's life: Miracle on the Water and Miracle of the Putting Out of the Novgorod Fire. The first scene refers to a legend about how St. Basil saved a Persian ship in the Caspian Sea. During a horrible storm, Orthodox Christians, who were on the ship along with Persians, were praying for salvation. Suddenly they saw a naked man walking on the water, who pacified the sea. When the travelers came to Moscow, they recognized Basil the Blessed as their savior. According to another legend, the Czar offered Basil a goblet of wine three times, and Basil would

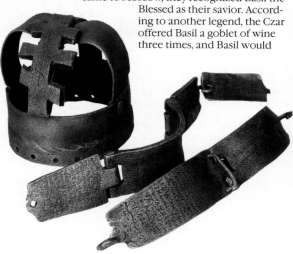

The heavy iron cap and fetters of John the Blessed

Cathedral Chapels, their Altar Holidays and Significance
(all dates given according to the new calendar)

1 **Central Chapel of the Intercession of the Holy Virgin** (October 14), protector of all Christians and celestial patron of Russia.

2. **Northern Chapel of the Holy Martyrs Cyprian and Justina** (October 15): the storming and fall of Kazan.

3. **Northeastern Chapel of the Three Patriarchs of Constantinople: Alexander, John and Paul the New** (September 12): Russians defeated a large Tartar troop led by Prince Epancha.

4. **Eastern Chapel of the Holy Trinity** (Holy Trinity Day): glory to Our Lord.

5. **Southeastern Chapel of St. Alexander of Svir** (September 12): Russians defeated a large Tartar troop led by Prince Epancha.

6. **Southern Chapel of St. Nicholas Velikoretsky** (May 22, December 19): the revelation of a new miracle-working icon as a sign of St. Nicholas' blessing of the Czar.

7. **Southwestern Chapel of St. Varlaam of Khutyn** (November 19): possibly, in memory of Vasily III, Ivan the Terrible's father. In his old age, Vasily III followed the tradition of Russian rulers and became a monk under the name of Varlaam.

8. **Western Chapel of the Entry of Our Lord into Jerusalem** (Palm Sunday): the cathedral's symbolism as a new Jerusalem, both earthly and heavenly.

9. **Northwestern Chapel of the Holy Martyr Gregory, the Bishop and Enlightener of Armenia** (October 13): a part of the Kazan fortress wall and Arsk tower captured.

10. **St. Basil the Blessed Church.**

11. **Belfry.**

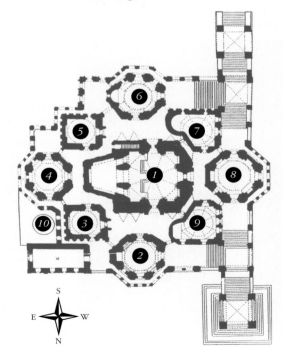

dump the wine on the ground every time. When the Czar demanded an explanation, Basil claimed he had just put out a great fire in Novgorod. Some time later, Novgorodians confirmed they had seen a naked man who put out a major fire in their town with water.

There is another — more gruesome — tale frequently associated with the images of St. Basil. One of Basil's rich worshippers once convinced him to accept an expensive fur coat as a gift. Some thieves decided to cheat Basil out of his fur coat. One of them feigned death, while the others asked Basil to donate something for their friend's funeral. Basil covered the alleged dead body with his fur coat, saying: "Be dead now for your lies." When Basil left, the thieves lifted up the coat and saw that their co-conspirator was, indeed, dead.

St. Basil's Church did not have a passage to the main temple until the 19th century. This is now the public entry to the Cathedral basement. The niches in the basement used to be depositories where a part of the royal treasury was stored. Centuries ago, locals also stored their valuables here. The Cathedral's thick stone walls offered reliable protection from fires, which happened quite frequently in Moscow. It was not easy to get into the basement, which has no windows. The only access was a narrow staircase leading down

Façade Icon of the Protection of the Holy Virgin with John and Basil the Beatific on the southern belfry wall

from the second level. This is the staircase visitors use to climb to the second-level Chapeles and walk around the cathedral through a wraparound indoor gallery. Admiring the murals, one should bear in mind that they were painted at different — relatively recent — times. The original painting was plain brickwork.

1. The Chapel of the Intercession of the Holy Virgin (main Chapel)

This Chapel was one of the earliest architectural experiments that placed two octagons sharing a ribbed roof on top of a square. This started a whole new trend in architecture. However, a tall structure like this with a small base plate is very difficult to heat, and cannot be used by many people praying at the same time, which is one of the reasons why very few churches like this were ever built.

The iconostasis now standing inside the Chapel of the Intercession of the Holy Virgin was transferred here in 1770 from the Chernigov Church inside the Kremlin after it was divested of its church status. The old iconostasis was sold to the village of Svistukha in the Kaliazin region for 70 rubles. The central Chapel icon — The Intercession of the Holy Virgin — dates back to that time, as do the other icons in this

Confession by the Shrine of St. Basil the Blessed, 19th century

Chapel, including several images of Basil the Blessed.

The interior of the Chapel is decorated with restored 16th century murals. High above (the Chapel is 47.5 m tall), under the rotunda windows, the builders had inscribed the date when the Cathedral was completed: 29 June (Julian calendar) 1561. The southerly wall displays some 19th century icon art, and there is a fragment of an 18th century mural in the southwesterly corner.

2. The Chapel of the Holy Martyrs Cyprian and Justina (northern Chapel)

The iconostasis of the Chapel of Sts. Cyprian and Justina was created in 1784–1786, and its icons were painted at the same time. The icons in the bottom row tell the story of the two days of the Creation, when the Lord created water and the sky.

The murals display scenes of suffering from the life of Sts. Cyprian and Justina (second row), and Sts. Adrian and Natalia (first row). The images of the latter two martyrs were painted in 1786, when a certain Natalia Khrushcheva, a wealthy parishioner, donated money for repair and, in return, asked for the Chapel to be rededicated in her honor. Her wish was granted, but the original dedication was eventually restored. An image of Virgin Mary looks down from the Chapel dome.

This Chapel houses two metal church gonfalons. One, bearing the image of Our Savior Facing Sergius of Radonezh and Varlaam of Khutyn, was introduced in 1913 in celebration of the 300th anniversary of the House of Romanov. The other, displaying

Early 20th century watercolor of the iconostasis of the Chapel of the Intercession of the Holy Virgin

the Intercession of the Holy Virgin with the namesake saints of members of the royal family, was placed in the Chapel in 1904 on the occasion of the birth of Prince Alexius.

3. The Chapel of the Three Patriarchs of Constantinople: Alexander, John and Paul the New (northeastern Chapel)

The five-level iconostasis at the Three Patriarchs' Chapel was created in 1842–1849. In 1849, this Chapel was rededicated to St. Gregory of Armenia, which explains why the murals in the top row represent the life of the three Patriarchs of Constantinople, while the murals in the bottom row display scenes from the life of St. Gregory, the Enlightener of Armenia.

Cruciform vaulted ceiling at St. Basil's Church

Dome of the Chapel of the Holy Trinity

4. The Chapel of St. Nicholas (southern Chapel)

The original iconostasis of the Chapel of St. Nicholas burned down in the 1737 fire; the existing one was crafted in 1786. The Chapel icons date back to the same time, including the main icon of St. Nicholas of Velikoretskoe on the southern door of the iconostasis.

House Icon of the Holy Trinity (16th century) in the Trinity Chapel, one of the earliest surviving icons belonging to the Cathedral of the Intercession

The 19th century murals illustrate a story from a Nikon-era chronicle about how the Icon of St. Nicholas of Velikoretskoe was brought to Moscow. The text on the northwestern wall tells the story of how the icon was received.

Most of the floors in this Chapel are covered with 18th century white stone slabs, but on one part of the floor, the slabs have been intentionally removed to expose the original oak parquet.

5. The Chapel of the Holy Trinity (eastern Chapel)

The iconostasis at the Holy Trinity Chapel has been restored in its 16th century look, incorporating coeval icons by Moscow and Novgorod painters. The main icon — 16th century Icon of the Holy Trinity — is one of the oldest existing icons at the Cathedral of the Intercession.

The architecture and decorations in this Chapel were also restored in their original 16th century look.

6. The Chapel of the Entry of Our Lord into Jerusalem (western Chapel)

The iconostasis of the Chapel of the Entry of Our Lord into Jerusalem was moved here in 1770 from the Kremlin Church of St. Alexander Nevsky, abolished three years earlier. The majority of the icons in this Chapel were painted in the 18th century, but there are two 17th century icons here that are quite unique. One is the Icon of St. Alexander Nevsky with 33 scenes from his life, showing the holy and virtuous prince in his monastic vestments. Shortly before his death, Prince Alexander Nevsky took monastic vows and the name Alexius. The second icon, depicting the Entry of Our Lord into Jerusalem, may have been moved here from another major church in the Kremlin.

The interior of this Chapel is exactly the same as it was in the 17th century.

7. The Chapel of St. Alexander of Svir (southeastern Chapel)

At the Chapel of St. Alexander of Svir, the conjoined iconostasis has been restored in its original 16th century look, featuring an assortment of 16th and 17th century icons. The dominant image is an early 18th century

Restored late 17th century murals in the wraparound indoor gallery

icon of St. Alexander of Svir. Two sewed 18th century shrouds hang underneath the icon row.

The walls in this Chapel are painted to resemble brickwork, the same way they were in the 16th century.

8. The Chapel of St. Varlaam of Khutyn (south-western Chapel)

The two-level conjoined iconostasis of the Chapel of St. Varlaam of Khutyn has been restored in its 16th century look, consisting of 16th–18th century icons, two of them completely unique: the 16th century icons of St. Varlaam of Khutyn and Vision of Sexton Tarasius. The latter icon illustrates a legend about how the late St. Varlaam appeared before Tarasius, the sexton at the Khutyn Monastery, to predict the fire and famine to be visited on Novgorod for its sins in 1508. The saint also predicted a great flood, but the flood never happened thanks to St. Varlaam's intervention before the Lord.

The whitewashed walls look exactly the same as they did in the 17th century.

9. The Chapel of the Holy Martyr Gregory, Bishop and Enlightener of Armenia (northwestern Chapel)

The restored conjoined iconostasis in the Chapel of St. Gregory of Armenia houses several 17th century icons by different painters, as well as a 16th century icon of John the Merciful. In 1788, a wealthy parishioner named Ivan Kislinsky had the Chapel rededicated in the name of St. John the Merciful, the Patriarch of Alexandria.

Cathedral Symbolism

It is not easy to unravel all the symbolism built by the old architects into a temple erected so many centuries ago, but we can guess a few things.

The four tall pillar Chapeles around the central temple face the four parts of the

Cathedral of the Intercession, 18th century

world, while the four lower Chapeles are positioned symmetrically in between. This suggests that the old architects designed the cathedral as two squares, one inside the other with a 45 degree shift. This shape forms an eight-pronged star, one of the symbols of the Holy Virgin usually displayed on her robes. The same star is repeated in the layout of the octagonal tent-like roof of the Chapel of the Intercession. It is believed that the nine-dome temple is in itself a symbol of Our Lady as a celestial patron of the Russian Orthodox Church. The cathedral is filled with Virgin Mary symbolism.

Another set of symbolism is linked to the concept of Moscow as "The Third Rome" and heir to the former hubs of Orthodox Christianity, which gained circulation during the reign of Ivan the Terrible. Moscow was to become an agglomeration of sanctity, saints and sacred objects. The Cathedral of the Intercession with its many onion domed Chapeles that look like a small town in its own right was conceived as a symbol of the earthly and heavenly city of Jerusalem.

After a 72-year silence, the bells of the Cathedral of the Intercession chimed again on 14 October 1990, Day of the Intercession of the Holy Virgin